NMS PUBLISHING PRESENTS ...

SCOTTISH SHOWBUSINESS

MUSIC HALL, VARIETY AND PANTOMIME

DEVISED AND WRITTEN
BY FRANK BRUCE

All captions credited 'Scottish Life Archive'
are held at the National Museums of Scotland.

Published by NMS Publishing Limited
National Museums of Scotland
Chambers Street, Edinburgh EH1 1JF

Series editor: Iseabail Macleod

British Library Cataloguing in Publication Data
A catalogue record of this book
is available from the British Library.

Every effort has been made to trace the copyright owners of the material
included in this book. If any error or oversight has occurred the Publisher would be
grateful for information, and will correct any such error at the earliest opportunity.

ISBN 1-901663-43-4

Designed by Mark Blackadder.
Printed and bound in the United Kingdom by Bell and Bain Limited, Glasgow.

ACKNOWLEDGEMENTS

My thanks to Linda Fuchs for her support and advice and to all those who helped with this book:

Betty Brandon, Betty Clarkson, Stuart Eydmann, Archie Foley, Mac Fyfe, Paul Iles, Helen Kemp, Brian Kirk, Tulloch McDade, Janet McBain, Vikki MacDonnell, John McKillop, Hugh and Betty McLauchlan, Iseabail Macleod, Morven Muir, June Don Murray, Lena Nicol, Jim Pratt, Cara Shanley, Lesley Taylor and Mac Wilson – and also to those who have generously helped in my researches over the years, in particular Scottish music hall historian Jimmy Littlejohn and including Bill Abbott, Arthur Allen, Bob Bain, Margaret Bennett, William Brittel, Frank (snr) and Morag Bruce, Colin Calder, Billy Crockett, Frank Duffy, Charles Friell, Irene Fyfe, Will Fyffe Jnr, Billy Grey, Georgie Giddings, George Gillespie, Mabel Hall, Dave Hunter, Gordon Irving, George Johnstone, Jane Lindsay, Fran Lumsden, Muriel Mars, Larry Marshall, Bill McLenaghan, Adam MacNaughton, Primrose Milligan, May Morrison, Jack Richmond, Jim Smith, Al Stewart, Elizabeth Watson and George Woolley.

Thanks also to archivists and librarians:

Aberdeen City Library, Dundee Central Library, Dundee City Archives, Dunfermline Carnegie Library, Edinburgh City Library, Edinburgh City Archives, Inverness Library, Kirkwall Library, Leith Lives, Mitchell Library Glasgow, Motherwell Library, Trustees of the National Library of Scotland, School of Scottish Studies, Scottish Community Drama Association, Scottish Screen, Springburn Museum, Stirling Central Library.

Grateful acknowledgements to those who supplied pictures from private collections:

Douglas Campbell (p 25), Billy Crockett (p 128), Archie Foley (pp 33, 40, 50, 64, 83), Irene Fyfe (p 114), Mabel Hall (pp 65, 67, 87, 112), Jane Lindsay (p 119), John McKillop (p 41), Hugh and the late Betty McLauchlan (pp 90, 111), the late May Morrison (pp 45, 46, 104, 116, 132), Morven Muir (p 84), June Don Murray (facing title right, p 130 top) and Jim Pratt (pp 23, 24, 93).

An earlier version of chapter 3 appeared in the journal *Scotlands* (5 January 1998) and of chapter 11 in *Theatre Notebook* (volume LII no. 2, 1999).

Illustrations (page ii)
Left: Johnny Victory, who specialised in comical, topical and sentimental monologues in the 1950s and '60s, in particular a top-hat and tails French turn, '*Pierre ze great lovaire*'. (May Morrison)

Right: Jack Beattie, champion Scottish Highland dancer and variety theatre all-rounder. Portrait by Roy Don, manager of the Palladium, Edinburgh, who produced them for performers to have made into publicity postcards and for the Palladium foyer.

'Double Scotch', an ENSA (Entertainments National Service Association) concert party
produced by Falkirk showman Dave Hunter and partner Bert Dixon,
on stage during a tour of the Middle East. Many Scottish performers spent the World War II years
entertaining the troops. Dave Hunter had, like many of his generation, launched his performing career
in a World War I army concert party. The cast are (*left to right*): Dave Hunter, Bert Dixon, Billy Sellers (pianist),
unidentified acrobat and dancer, Margaret Smart (violinist), Gibson Sisters and Buddy, Cathy Meik (accordion).
(Source: School of Scottish Studies/Dave Hunter)

CONTENTS

Strongwomen spieling outside a booth at the Jooley Fair, Milnathort, in the 1940s. Held on the 4th Monday in July, the Jooley Fair was the main event of the year, with special trains laid on to bring visitors. This is a late example of the booths once common at fairs. The Jooley Fair dwindled and finally stopped in 1977. (Scottish Life Archive)

A street showman by the Twa Brigs in Ayr – humble exhibitors thronged
busy nineteenth-century thoroughfares, in this case with some sort of portable 'diorama',
probably containing a three-dimensional
painting with lighting effects.
(*The Land of Burns*, Glasgow 1840)

INTRODUCTION

Recollections of Scottish showbusiness often invoke a golden age with which the present cannot compete. There is nothing new about this. One commentator in 1856 described a Mr McGregor, then appearing at the Paisley music hall, as 'a favourite comedian nearly a quarter of a century ago … who yet sings comic songs with a spirit which might put scores of younger vocalists to the blush'. Almost 40 years later another 'Old Growler' complained:

> The modern pro must have all the paraphernalia appertaining to the business – grease paints, rouge, lining-pencils, and so forth, and a mammoth basket full of character costumes. The old times pro could get ready in two minutes; the present-day pro cannot do it in under half an hour. The former was funny in himself, the latter is ludicrous with the aid of multitudinous 'properties'.

A century on, another columnist is saying much the same thing, this time lamenting the lack of new comic talent: 'It would be nice to think there are new Logans, Fultons, Baxters and Radcliffes waiting in the wings but I'll believe it when I see it.'

Such nostalgia reflects the relentless change that has occurred in the entertainment business during the past two centuries. In 1800 showbusiness was sporadic, small-scale and locally organised, largely unaltered for generations and catering to a predominantly rural population. At the turn of the millennium, commercialised entertainment has become all-pervasive and international, and it is constantly evolving.

The age of mass-entertainment in music halls and variety theatres in Scotland (and across Europe and North America) occupies a halfway position in this evolution and illustrates with particular clarity the mix of continuity and innovation, the confrontation between local culture and unfolding 'globalisation' that continues to shape popular entertainment.

Leith Races by William Reed, *circa* 1850s.
Victorian local historian William Hutchison describes the 200 year-old races as having
a 'multitude of minor amusements .... These consisted of shows, wheels of fortune, and rowley-powley
[a form of ninepins played at fairs] in endless variety, and last, though not the least, whole streets
of drinking-booths and tents ... for an entire week the town was one continued scene of racing, drinking,
and fighting; and the sports were usually concluded by a general demolition of the booths ... '.
Hutchison expressed typical mid-Victorian satisfaction when the races were finally closed in 1856.
(Edinburgh City Art Centre)

FROM FAIRS TO FREE AND EASIES

In the early nineteenth century much popular entertainment in Scotland focused around the calendar of fairs. These had declined in agricultural importance since the end of the previous century, but the entertainment element, if anything, grew. Showpeople moved around the country from fair to fair, hiring whatever venues they could in between, and exhibiting many of the acts later gathered together in music hall. William Tennant's poem 'Anster Fair' (1811) lists the acts at Anstruther fair as including 'tumblers in wondrous pranks', 'motley Merry-Andrew, with his jokes', as well as open-air players in 'Davie Lindsay's plays' and ballad-singing women.

Such entertainers had been in Scotland for centuries and Tennant's poem belonged – quite self-consciously – to a tradition recording their presence that stretches back through Robert Ferguson's 'Leith Races' to the sixteenth-century ballad 'Peblis to the Play'. At the same time, changes in the nature and scale of entertainments heralded broader transformation. Literary acknowledgement of this link can be found in Galt's fictional social history, *Annals of the Parish*, where the Reverend Micah Balwhidder mentions the establishment of a fair in 1770 as seeing the arrival of more 'more mountebanks and Merry Andrews now, and richer cargoes of groceries and packman's stands' and the debut in the village of a Punch and Judy show:

> … *O he was a sorrowful contumacious captain, and it was just a sport to see how he rampaged, and triumphed, and sang. For months after, the laddie weans did nothing but squeak and sing.*

For Galt's narrator the arrival of professional entertainers in his rural parish was a symptom of encroaching change, and, indeed, from the end of the eighteenth century the proliferation of all types of amusements ran in parallel with the unfolding agricultural and industrial revolutions.

The seasonal fair tradition was continued by showpeople like Billy Purvis (a Geordie, but born in Achendinny near Edinburgh) who toured the north of England and the Scottish Lowlands throughout the 1820s and '30s. In 1824 he set up his *Fantocini* (puppet) theatre in a Kelso blacksmith's, going on to take a lease on the Kelso Theatre until 1825, then moving to Jedburgh where he erected a wooden and canvas booth. He hired a blind fiddler, bought a clown's dress which was 'sadly too short in the breeches' and painted his face 'all colours', but did not draw the crowds until he played a few tunes on his Northumbrian pipes. From Jedburgh he moved to Edinburgh and then to Musselburgh races. In 1826 he embarked on another tour of the Lowlands, having taken on a small company of actors. At Kilmarnock Fair his pitch was opposite that of an Italian named Codoni who, as he puts it, with his family 'displayed their feats of tumbling and postures extraordinary'. From Kilmarnock they went to Paisley Fair and then to Dundee.

The lot of these entertainers was a hard one, many being little more than buskers, often elderly, ill or disabled and a step away from destitution. In a series of articles in *Chambers' Journal* entitled 'Life's undercurrent', the author narrates his precarious youthful career as an orphan in the 1820s, first leading a blind fiddler and singing popular Scots songs for two years, and then joining a small band of showpeople specialising in singing Italian songs:

> *We were too poor to pay for our conveyance by coach, so we set off on foot, each carrying his own instrument, and Leonora [the soprano] her bundle of dresses. I had a good share of the burthen myself – all the bills that were to be posted up when we made a halt at any place where we hoped to collect an audience, and the little linen my master and mistress had … and towards the evening I was often ready to sink under it. We were ever in difficulties, for our expenses were certain, and our audiences very uncertain ….*

The troupe soon broke up when Leonora ran off with the cash and linen.

In the swelling cities there were a growing number of more permanent attractions. Robert Chambers remembered Edinburgh's Leith Walk in the 1810s as 'a scene of wonders and enjoyments' from top to bottom. Apart from the transient panoramas and caravan-shows

> *… there were several shows upon Leith Walk, which might be considered as regular fixtures ….*

Who can forget the wax-works of 'Mrs Sands, widow of the late G. Sands,' which occupied a laigh [basement] *shop opposite to the present Haddington Place, and at the door of which, besides various parrots, and the sundry birds of Paradise, sat the wax figure of a little man in the dress of a French courtier of the* ancien regime, *reading one eternal copy of the* Edinburgh Advertiser!

Travelling showfolk rented rooms in hotels or over pubs, or more spacious public 'exhibition rooms'. On her first visit to Scotland in June 1803 Madame Tussaud exhibited her 'accurate models from life' in Glasgow's New Assembly Hall, Ingram Street after a successful appearance in Laurie's Room, Thistle Street, Edinburgh:

> *… I have found everything is going well. For example today is the 18th our waxworks have been opened and we have taken £190. 1s. …. Next July we are going to have the fair and the horse show which lasts a fortnight. Everybody will come to Capital from the Provinces and the Country and we hope to have a bumper fortnight.*

Less successful was Giovanni Belzoni, a former Capuchin monk from Padua. He had come to England hoping to make his fortune with his inventions in hydraulics, but was forced instead to make a living as a travelling strongman and, a few months before Madame Tussaud in 1803, hired public rooms in Edinburgh where he was noticed by Egyptologist Henry Salt (who in 1815, after a chance re-meeting in Egypt, employed Belzoni's hydraulic services in the removal of several large statues which ended up in the British Museum):

> *One day in the beginning of 1803, Mr. Salt observed before one of the public rooms of Edinburgh, a great crowd assembled …. There, on a sort of stage, he saw a tall and powerfully-built young man, performing various gymnastic exercises, and feats of strength. While this Hercules in tinsel was lifting enormous weights, and jumping from a table over the heads of twelve men, a pretty, delicate-looking young woman was arranging some hydraulic machines and musical glasses, with which the entertainment was to terminate. As the price of admission was nominal, she occasionally also handed round a small wooden bowl, in order to collect gratuities from the spectators. Very few of those who were enjoying the exhibition gave any thing; and when the young woman approached her husband, and showed him the few coins she had received, he hastened to terminate his performance.*

Leases might also be taken on permanent theatres (for example, in addition to the Kelso Theatre, Billy Purvis mentions taking the lease

Buffalo Bill's Wild West Show visiting Ayr in September 1904 during a four-year tour of Europe. Early circuses had tended to be in permanent structures but, following the fashion imported from America, large, spectacular touring tented circuses and menageries began to tour from the mid-nineteenth century, notably the British Bostock and Wombwell's menagerie which came to Scotland in 1873 and made regular tours thereafter. (Scottish Life Archive)

wells); 'Monstrosities' (including a visit by Tom Thumb to the County Rooms in 1846); 'Conjurors' (including Signor Belzoni in December 1810, 'who declared that he learned his tricks from the Chinese .... He announced that he would cut off a cock's head and put it on again'); 'Ventriloquists' (such as Carmichael, who in January 1832 performed in the hall of Machray's Hotel); 'Mechanisms' of various kinds; 'Panoramas' and 'Various Entertainments' including lectures, orrerys (clockwork models of the planets), 'philosophical fireworks', 'performances on the musical glasses', and waxworks.

Growing urban audiences attracted entrepreneurial showpeople and many of the major circus families toured Scotland from the start of the century – one of many shifts putting showbusiness on a more organised, capital-intensive footing. Modern circus had developed in London towards the end of the previous century, and unlike the familiar tented circus, early circuses were generally in permanent theatre-like buildings. The first circus in Edinburgh, the New Sadler's Well's Theatre, was opened by riding masters George Jones and William Parker in 1790, and in 1794 Jones opened another Circus building in Glasgow. By the 1840s the Cookes, Sangers and Henglers were regular visitors with pitches in the major cities. One of the most famous circus person-

of Cooke's Circus in Dundee and Greenock Theatre for a spell in the late 1830s), or semi-permanent booths would be built. The range of venues and amusements is well illustrated in 'How our Grandfathers amused themselves – Some account of the shows that used to visit Aberdeen' in *Scottish Notes and Queries* (June 1901). The author reviews a collection of old posters from the first decades of the nineteenth century under the following headings – 'Menageries' (including several visits by the famous Womb-

alities of the time, equestrian performer Andrew Ducrow, had established 'Amphitheatres' in Edinburgh, Glasgow and Aberdeen during the 1820s and '30s. The latter, Ducrow's Royal Amphitheatre and Arena (opened in 1830) was, it seems, a substantial affair with a tiled roof, brilliant lighting inside, a pit, gallery and row of boxes and, according to the second night's bill, it was capable of holding over 2000 spectators.

Assortments of wooden circuses, theatres and more booths sprang up on urban waste ground across Scotland. In Glasgow they clustered around the Saltmarket, including the well-remembered song, dance and puppetry of Bedfordshire puppeteer Mumford's Mechanical Theatre built at the foot of the Saltmarket in the 1830s. In 1839 David Prince Miller, a showman from London who had worked in menageries and as a conjuror and fire-eater, arrived in Glasgow from Dalkeith after a tour of the Borders. He gives a vivid sense of the highly competitive showman's world:

> My whole stock of cash was exhausted in defraying the expenses of this journey. Two horses were required to convey my concern; and what with their hire, turnpikes, &c, some six or seven pounds were expended. I procured a site to erect my booth. There were plenty of exhibitions at this fair; and I must acknowledge that mine was, in appearance, the least in consequence of them all. I therefore was not very sanguine as to my success, and did not anticipate making a fortune. Mr. J. H. Anderson, the Great Wizard of the North, as he termed himself, was at the same fair; he had a most magnificent building erected for the display of his legerdemain. His principle experiment was the gun trick, which at that time was most attractive. This experiment I had long since discontinued; but observing the success which attended Mr. Anderson's exhibition I, too, performed the gun trick; my charge was one penny, Mr. A.'s sixpence. He was rather chagrined at my opposing him, and noticed me in his harrangues to the crowd, and also by innuendos in his bills – a proceeding that advanced my interest materially. Had he been wise he would not have noticed me. To be brief. After the fair, I was in possession of upwards of seventy pounds.

Their gradual encroachment of these booths and theatres onto Glasgow Green led to an 1845 movement and a 60,000-signature petition to get rid of them.

The boundaries between high and low theatre, circus and spectacle were still remarkably fluid (both Miller and Anderson ventured into dramatic presentations). Cheek by jowl with travelling menageries, more dramatic diversions could be found in the small 'gaffs' specialising in short episodes from Shakespeare or Scottish

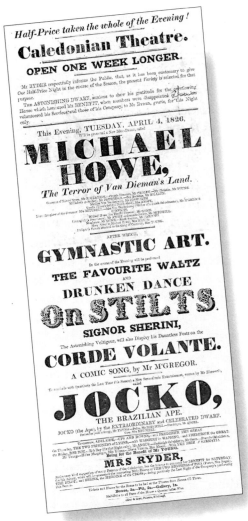

The Caledonian Theatre had previously been a concert hall and ballroom, and before that a circus. As we can see, an extraordinarily wide range of diversions were presented in the early nineteenth century 'minor' theatres. (National Library of Scotland)

literature, or in larger 'Penny Geggies' (portable timber and canvas theatres), with a repertoire of more substantial melodrama and the Walter Scott adaptations and imitations known as 'national drama'.

In Dundee, Fizzy Gow's Gaff was run by James Gow, a tailor with a taste for the theatre. Out of work and living in Edinburgh, he set up a tiny 'Theatre Royal' in Grey's Close, consisting of a bed turned into a stage, with the bed-curtains as drapes. A similar venture in an old dressing loft in Dundee had greater success, followed by slightly more elaborate premises near the Overgate. This also doubled as home, with pots and pans being stowed behind the stage during performances:

The antiquated bed curtains … were dispensed with, and two painted scenes, in which the perspective was omitted, substituted in their place. One of these was utilised as the 'drop', or curtain, while the other, which was supposed to represent a picturesque landscape was at different times during the performance of a piece used for the indiscriminate purposes of a drawing-room, a prison, a gloomy dungeon keep, or a bower …. The footlights, two penny candles, which for the sake of economy had been cut through the middle, cast a dim halo of light around the room. An old fiddler, generally blind, supplied the orchestral accompaniment. The pieces

generally performed were 'Rob Roy', 'The Castle Spectre', 'The Wreck Ashore', 'The Gentle Shepherd', and the tragedy of 'Douglas', although when an occasional star or tramp came round and made Mr Gow's abode his headquarters, 'Richard the Third', Macbeth', and even 'Hamlet' were performed.

Another move followed to larger premises in the Nethergate, but through the 1850s trade started to decline, and Gow ended his career in Dundee with a small booth of 'automatic figures'. On his death he bequeathed his theatrical wardrobe to music-hall and theatre impresario William MacFarland, of whom more later.

Music hall was to draw much of its business and performing talent from all these sources and there was no straightforward evolution from any one of them; portable theatres, spectaculars and sideshows continued alongside for decades, and in the case of circus, right up to the present. But the most obvious predecessors for the purpose-built music halls and the music-hall performers were to be found in the unlicensed and licensed theatres (licensed to present plays) and the 'free and easies' or 'singing saloons' which appeared in towns and cities across Scotland and the rest of the United Kingdom in the 1830s and '40s.

Licensed theatres and their other non-'legit' competitors shared a great deal in the first half

Conjurors had progressed from the streets and private salons to the theatre stage towards the end of the eighteenth century. Swiss Monsieur Chalon, here appearing in the Pantheon Theatre (formerly the Caledonian), arrived in England in 1820. The 'transformation of a bird into a young lady' was one of his trademark illusions. (National Library of Scotland)

of the nineteenth century, not least audiences. Theatres habitually incorporated song, dance, musical and spectacular elements into dramatic programmes, which they puffed in playbills in an attempt to lure audiences from the growing number of other attractions, particularly circuses and unlicensed 'minor' theatres, but not always with success. In 1831 the lessees of Dundee Theatre Royal brought a 'good company' to the theatre on 31 December, and subsequently produced the first regular pantomime in Dundee, but the people preferred Ord's Circus, then performing in the Meadows.

Conversely, circus incorporated various 'sub-dramatic' burletta, pantomimic and ballet elements, as well as tumbling, juggling, rope dancing, equestrian and other animal perform-ances. Moreover, it was common for circus per-formers to appear in theatres. This might be as an interlude in dramatic programmes, or as a whole show: in 1828 Andrew Ducrow made two appearances at Glasgow Theatre Royal, where the manager had the pit torn up to make an arena in order to stage one of Ducrow's 'hippocratic melodramas'. In Edinburgh in 1837 he even appeared in the Theatre Royal as an actor (to favourable reviews) for seven appearances, after finishing the evening's work at his own 'Arena' on Nicholson Street. Many theatres were effectively given over to proto-variety bills. The

New Theatre, in the former Perth Grammar School building, had as part of its 1810 opening farces, melodramas, Signor Belzoni in 'Feats of Strength' and tunes on the musical glasses, and Herman Boaz's 'Thaumaturgical [ie wonder-working] Exhibitions and Magical Deceptions'.

Turning to the 'singing saloons' and 'free and easies', the terms cover two distinct but over-lapping entities. On the one hand were pubs which gave a room or two over to amateur entertainments, often organised around the numerous social clubs of the period, with solo turns by members and chorus 'glees'. On the other hand a more regular programme might be established, and professional singers, often drawn from the theatre stage, might be engaged in addition to the amateurs.

These glorified pubs were part of the mid-Victorian pub boom, yet were another façet of a general commercialisation of leisure. Some were expensively fitted up to attract businessmen, but most provided a more basic environment for shopkeepers, clerks and artisans, with entrance gained by purchase of a drink and entertainment consisting of popular songs of the day, rendered from a raised platform with a pianist. According to future music-hall star W F Frame, recollecting such Glasgow saloons as the Crystal Palace and Sam's Chop House in Glasgow, 'Anyone who was bold enough could make an appearance at

Burning of the City Theatre,
Glasgow, 1845.
This was one of several substantial
wooden 'minor' theatres at the foot of
the Saltmarket. According to one
account, the proprietor, magician
J H Anderson, who was only partially
insured and would not recoup his
investment, 'would have rushed into
the flames in the hope of saving some
of his property if he had not been
restrained'. Fires were a regular hazard
and by 1849 the Adelphi and Cooke's
circus had been destroyed in Glasgow
and 70 lives lost in a panic at the
Theatre Royal.
(*Illustrated London News*)

such a concert, his friends doing the needful by handing his or her name to the chairman, who, like the pianist, was paid at the rate of 5/- per night'.

In Edinburgh, John Wilson McLaren (a former patron) described these as springing up 'mushroom-like', mainly in the most densely populated parts of the city, with almost any pub that had a back-room setting up in business. He recalls Bryce's on Princes Street and White's at the top of the North Bridge as long subter-ranean rooms, with the proceedings regulated by a chairman with his hammer. Mother Anderson's, 'a favourite rendezvous of the Auld Reekie printers', seems to fall into the amateur convivial category:

Here only Saturday night 'free-and-easies' were
held. Musical talent was always strongly developed
among Auld Reekie printers, and the frequenters
of Mother Anderson's could always rely on a good
night's entertainment.

Before and after the chapel was built, Aberdeen.
This graphic illustration of the supposed evil consequences of popular entertainment, though an exaggerated comparison, nonetheless suggests the impact the arrival of a travelling fit-up must have had in otherwise entertainment-free neighbourhoods. As the nineteenth century progressed, churches tended to be turned into places of entertainment, rather than the reverse. (Scottish Life Archive)

The move to distinct music halls providing more varied programmes was largely a matter of supply and demand, but had been accelerated in Scotland, as elsewhere around the United Kingdom, by the Theatre Act of 1843. This was the culmination of long-running friction between licensed theatres and the unlicensed entertainment purveyors whom licensees felt were poaching their audiences by illicitly presenting drama (notably in the case of Glasgow licensee J H Alexander, prosecuting both David Prince Miller and magician J H Anderson). The Act forced a choice between staging plays and not having refreshments in the auditorium, or serving refreshments and not staging plays, or in other words presenting a largely musical entertainment. This was the choice of Jupiter Saloon, a 'temperance hall' in Glasgow described by an 1858 visitor:

As we enter, a song is being sung, 'Anything for a Crust.' The artiste, dressed in appropriate habiliments, is vociferously applauded. The curtain drops, and, as before, a scene takes place among 'the gods,' who are in number upwards of a hundred or so. They consist chiefly of working lads from twelve to twenty, with a slight sprinkling of another class, of both sexes, not quite so respectable. Fruit, ginger-beer, &c., are now handed round. The bell rings, and a smartly-dressed young English woman ascends the stage or platform; and, what with beauty and song, enraptures the audience. She pauses, smiles, and sings again, and finally retires amidst vociferous 'encores'.

The author 'Shadow', social reformer Alexander Brown, aimed, in his *Midnight scenes and social photographs* (1858), to expose the poverty and degradation of Glasgow's 'low life', which included popular leisure activities. How the growing urban working class spent its free time was a matter of great concern to middle-class social reformers. This drew on an older tradition of presbyterian objections to entertainers in general. In Stirling in the late 1840s, for example, William Drummond of the Stirling Tract Enterprise campaigned against the Sabbath-breaking occasioned by the lure of cheap fruit-picking and Sunday pubs in nearby Cambuskenneth, had the horse-racing closed down, and successfully agitated to have the travelling shows which set up on the castle esplanade (attracting trade from the barracks) moved. My own self-improving great-great-grandfather's recollection of his youthful leisure as a clerk in 1840s Glasgow reflected a prevailing attitude:

> *My office fellows often went to the theatre and sometimes to the tavern as I learnt from their talk. I went once or twice with them to the tavern and had a glass of ale, but latterly declined to go preferring a walk in Glasgow Green or a book in my lodgings. The theatre I abhorred from the descriptions I had heard of it and the ruin it brought on many I knew and I never entered its door ....*
> *I never wearied being alone as some of my acquaintances did and ran off to the theatre or singing saloons.*

Like Drummond's, my ancestor's opinion blended long-standing Knoxian sentiment with those of the increasingly active temperance movement. By 1854 this had taken organised form in the Glasgow Abstainers Union, devoted to providing counter-attractions to the public house with weekly City Hall Saturday Evening Concerts which were to continue for over 70 years. These, as we shall see, were to be a training ground for many future music-hall stars. For some, however, even temperance concerts were the devil's work. Gorbal's minister Robert Bremner attacked them in his 1857 sermon 'The Saturday Evening Concerts; A sin and a snare' – 19 pages of bible-bashing small print, repeatedly punctuated with Paul's warning to the Ephesians against 'filthiness nor foolish talking, nor jesting', and arguing that temperance concerts only whet appetites. Bremner had seen merely the beginnings of what was over the next few decades to become a music-hall boom.

Music Hall, Dunfermline,

ONE NIGHT ONLY.

A MERRY CHRISTMAS TO ALL.

Saturday Evening, Dec. 25, 1869.

THE GREATEST ATTRACTION EVER OFFERED!

☞ 2500 A CHRISTMAS PRESENT TO EVERY ONE.

COSTLY PRESENTS WILL BE GIVEN AWAY.

PROF. MILLAR,

The World-Renowned Illusionist, has the honour to announce his Wonderful, Extraordinary, Mysterious, Marvellous, Exciting, Surprising, and Curious ENTERTAINMENT, introducing the greatest BUDGET of Wonders ever witnessed.

CAPT. AUSTIN,

(Late U.S.A.) who will give his Astonishing ENTERTAINMENT in

VENTRILOQUISM!

Vocal Imitation, and Original Anecdotes, when he will imitate Bipeds and Quadrupeds, with specimens of

VOCAL ILLUSION

In conversation with Invisible Beings, introducing the Old Scotch Lady—Mrs JANET MACDOUGAL—

THE SPEAKING HAND!

Who will sing. "John Anderson my Joe, John," Smoke a Pipe, &c.

PADDY MURPHY'S OPINION,

With a Song.

John Brown's novel way of getting down from the Roof of the House. Thomas in the Hamper, a Song. Voices in the Cellar, on the House top, out at the Window; Voices here, there, and everywhere, with

IMITATIONS OF BARKING DOGS, &c.

Voices Human and Inhuman—Childish—Fiendish; the Noises of all Noisy Handicrafts, combining a fund of Wonder and Amusement of the most pleasing and astounding character, thus forming a

Grand Double Entertainment

At one Price of Admission.

On the above night there will be GIVEN AWAY to the Audience a Large Number of

COSTLY PRESENTS,

Exceeding anything ever attempted here, and will include—

SIX POUNDS IN MONEY.

TWO GOLD WATCHES,

One Splendid Time-piece,

With Glass Shade and Stand.

BEAUTIFUL CARD BASKETS,

One Silver-Plated

TEA AND COFFEE SERVICE,

GOLD BROOCHES, GOLD RINGS,

One Rich and

ELEGANT SILK DRESS,

SILVER DRINKING CUPS,

And many other Rich, Rare, and Valuable Articles, too numerous to mention, forming the most costly number of Gifts ever presented, all to be GIVEN AWAY in the strictly honourable manner which has given universal satisfaction in all parts of Scotland, the whole amounting to

£55

In Money and Value, all to be Presented Free to the Audience.

GRAND COMPETITIVE CONTEST.

On the above Night, in order to encourage Local Talent, a large SILVER GOBLET will be given to the best Sentimental Singer; a SILVER WATCH to the best Comic Singer. Persons intending to compete must send in their Names, addressed to CAPTAIN AUSTIN, care of W. CLARK & SON, Booksellers, before SATURDAY, at Four o'clock, P.M. Two or more must enter into any Competition for the above Prizes, Captain AUSTIN reserving the right to select from, and limit the number.

GRAND CONUNDRUM NIGHT.

A Magnificent SILVER-PLATED TEA SERVICE will be given as a Prize for the best ORIGINAL CONUNDRUM. To be decided by a Committee of Gentlemen selected by the Audience. Authors to be present, and Conundrums to be addressed to CAPTAIN AUSTIN, care of W. CLARK & SON, Booksellers, before SATURDAY, at Four o'clock, P.M.

Selections will be made from the most Popular SONGS and BALLADS.

ADMISSION—FRONT SEATS, One Shilling..............GALLERY and PROMENADE, Sixpence.

Doors open at Seven, to commence at Eight o'clock.

Part of the Presents may be seen at Mr JOHN BOSWELL'S, Boot and Shoe Manufacturer, 21 High Street. Tickets may be had at the Door. Entrance by Guildhall Street.

CAPT. AUSTIN, Proprietor.

W. CLARK & SON, Steam Printers, Dunfermline.

Handbill for the Music Hall, Dunfermline.
Talent competitions, particularly for singers,
were a staple on music-hall bills and part of a wider amateur network.
Highly puffed prizes have become ubiquitous on television.
(Dunfermline Carnegie Library)

SWELL HOUSES AND ROUGH HOUSES

Concert venues that were known as 'music halls' predated and overlapped the more popular venues appearing from the late 1840s. The 'Music Hall' which was tacked onto the back of the Assembly Rooms in George Street in 1843, where Mr Julien subsequently promoted a series of 'Grand Concerts', was one of several concert halls (Aberdeen Assembly Rooms [1820], Glasgow City Hall [1841] and Queens Rooms [1850]) built to meet the demand for upmarket recitals. More modest was the typical 'polite' daytime concert that was advertised in the *Stirling Journal* for 28 May 1858: 'Music Hall, Bridge of Allan. Grand Morning Concert with the celebrated Bearnais Singers and Spanish Minstrels from France.'

Among the newer popular music-hall venues there was considerable variation both in scale and scope, and to further confuse matters some halls presented the whole range of polite and popular daytime and evening fare. Clark's Music Hall (1852) in Dunfermline was a substantial edifice built in response to agitation in the city for a public hall. William Clark, a bookseller by trade with a genius for engineering, personally designed and supervised the construction of the property which contained three halls, the main one able to seat 2000 and fitted out as a theatre. Though music-hall acts and bills were presented, the general tone of the establishment was 'high class' and multi-purpose, with recitals, touring theatre companies, soirées, dances, festivals, lectures and political meetings.

On the other hand, the Apollo Music Hall in Paisley was typical of the many opportunistic ventures cashing in on the entertainment boom. Though it merited a mention in the *Glasgow Amateur Public Amusement Record & General Miscellany*, no. 5 (5 November 1856), it seems to have escaped the notice of the Paisley press.

Paisley: Apollo Music Hall – The old Saracen's Head Ball Room has recently been fitted up and opened as a Music Hall, under the management of Mr. E. Danvers. The establishment is conducted with a decided aim at respectability. Among the performers is Mr. McGREGOR whom many will remember as a favourite comedian nearly a quarter of a century ago, and who yet sings comic songs with a spirit which might put scores of younger vocalists to the blush.

By the end of the decade, however, substantial and distinctive purpose-built venues dedicated to providing for the urban working class were going up, in addition to the scores of more *ad hoc* venues. In Glasgow, Campbell's – better known as the Britannia (1857) – still partially survives in the Trongate as one of Scotland's oldest theatres. By 1875 this had been followed by the Scotia (1862), the Royal Music Hall (1866), Prince of Wales (1867) and Gaiety (1874). In Edinburgh we have the New Royal Alhambra (1862), Southminster (1863) and Gaiety (1875), and in Leith the Royal Music Hall (1865), Theatre Royal (1867) and New Star Music Hall (1874), as well as the Dundee Alhambra (1870) and the Aberdeen Alhambra (1875).

These theatres were centred in populous working-class neighbourhoods, often replacing older wooden theatres. The Henglers, however,

abandoned tented circuses on an Edinburgh site which they had occupied since 1820, in order to build the Southminster. To this extent there was a continuity with the past, particularly between music hall and circus. What was new was the scale of investment and, while many of those involved in the business were show or theatre people, local businessmen took an increasing role.

In the last three decades of the century this commercialisation intensified. Impresarios began to control two or three halls at once, enabling them to offer longer engagements and lure better artistes. Dundonian D S Mackay, for example, went from running penny gaffs in his home town to running the Albert Hall of Variety in Edinburgh, the Gaiety in Glasgow's Sauchiehall Street, and the Star Music Hall near Glasgow Cross. William MacFarland, a native of Burnley in Lancashire, progressed from his first public appearances in Dundee's Kinnaird Hall in the 1860s with a diorama show entitled 'The Holy Land', to acquiring the wooden hall previously owned by the Sanger circus family for whom he had acted as agent. When the wooden theatre was condemned as unsafe in 1870, he took on the Exchange Coffee Rooms and converted them to a music hall which he ran for 17 years. In conjunction, he also managed the Aberdeen Alhambra, a converted church building. In

1877 he branched into legitimate theatre, taking over the lease of the Theatre Royal from his father-in-law, and then that of Her Majesty's Theatre in Aberdeen. His name, according to his obituary in the 1898 *Dundee Yearbook*, became 'almost a household word in Dundee and Aberdeen'.

The general expansion of entertainment was not simply a matter of ever more substantial buildings. There was a proliferation of speculative venues of all sizes in converted churches and the like, often lasting just a few months, and all this in addition to the older and smaller venues which carried on alongside. For example, Bryce's 'free and easy' in Edinburgh continued for 30 years until 1896, and in Glasgow a 'miniature music hall' like David Brown's continued until 1887. Outside urban centres, music-hall entertainment came in the form of touring companies who travelled small village halls the length and breadth of Scotland. These companies maintained a venerable tradition of travelling entertainers, but the type of entertainment provided was increasingly professional, with mini music-hall bills being presented, albeit with a stronger contingent of Scottish song, dance and 'characteristic' sketches than was the norm.

Celebrated violinist James Scott Skinner began his professional career in 1855 aged 12 with 'Dr Marks' little Men', after seeing them

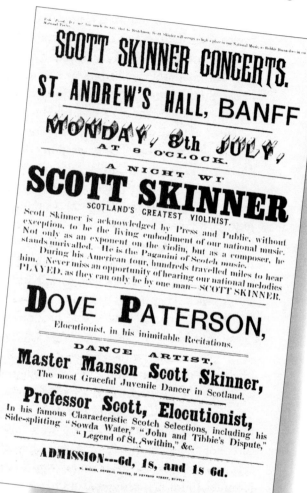

James Scott Skinner spent decades touring with the Scottish song, music and dance concert parties that were particularly popular round the North. 'Elocutionists' specialised in comic dialect recitations, and were popular well into the twentieth century. (Aberdeen City Libraries)

play in Aberdeen. He had visited about 600 towns and villages across Britain by the time he left four years later. Over the rest of his career he was frequently involved in touring concert parties in the north of Scotland and overseas, also making appearances on the music-hall stage.

Many of these touring shows were organised by 'Scotch' comedians. The biographies of four of them – James Houston, W F Frame, Harry Lauder and Neil McFadyen – dwell at length on their adventures touring rural Scotland. In July 1878 James Houston took part in James Lumsden's fifth tour of the north, with Miss Isa Robertson and his ten year-old son as the pianist, to Thurso, Castletown, Wick, Kirkwall and Lerwick. They had good houses and, with a small party, few expenses. The programme began with Master Lumsden playing a selection of Scotch airs on the piano dressed as a little Highlander, 'quite a favourite with the mammas and their young daughters'. Each of them then presented two turns in the first part of the programme, Master Lumsden playing an overture. For the second part they gave 'the now celebrated sketch of "Tam o' Shanter and Souter Johnnie", finishing up about 10.15 p.m., with a Scotch reel that sent the audience away in the best of spirits ...'.

Early in his career Lauder toured with several older comedians, and in particular with singer David Kennedy and his family going to Ayrshire, Dumfriesshire, round the Borders and up to the Central Belt:

> *At the larger towns, where they had a chance of hearing other travelling comedians, I was very successful, but at certain small places the people didn't seem to know whether to laugh or cry. So they did neither – just sat still, listened, and looked stupidly at me!*

In 1896 he toured with Banchory timber trader Donald Munro's North Concert party – a scheme organised by the part-time elocutionist and Scotch reciter to fill his long summer vacation. Lauder teamed up with the company's violinist Mackenzie Murdoch to organise their own tour in 1898, with 'Scott Rae, Caledonia's popular tenor; Flora Donaldson, brilliant soprano; and Howard, London's star ventriloquist' in addition to the two impresarios. The tour was a failure and cost the pair £100 each. At Stenhousemuir in Stirlingshire, where they played to eleven people and drew only one shilling and ninepence, an exasperated Lauder 'roundly rated' the inhabitants for not turning up in their hundreds to hear 'the finest concert party that ever toured the British Isles'. Small town and rural venues often proved unrewarding, perhaps due to a conservative religious bias against 'theatricals', or simply due to lack of spare money to spend. As *The Professional* noted in 1889:

> *The natives of Dunbar must be a dull race of people – we have repeatedly spoken about concertisers being frozen in that outlandish town, but only last week Miss Edith Clennell, a lady who can fill the St. Andrews Halls [Glasgow], gave one of her entertainments in Dunbar, and was rewarded with about a dozen of an audience. Poor Dunbar.*

In addition to touring, there were innumerable soirées, church bazaars, Burns suppers, football festivals and other functions offering employment. James Houston believed that he had 'been, at one time or other, with all the trades in Glasgow at their annual soirees'. One such annual soirée was for natives of Fife resident in Glasgow at the City Hall, for which, as was the practice, Houston specially wrote a topical song, 'The Hardy Sons of Fifeshire':

> *The Cellardyke and Pittenweem*
> *And Anster fishermen we've seen;*
> *Wrecked in the gales that's lately been*
> *Many lost their lives there.*
> *Then let us gie whit we can spare,*
> *To cheer the helpless mourners there,*
> *And the widows and the orphans' prayer,*
> *Will bless the sons of Fifeshire.*

These non music-hall concerts provided early training grounds for the novice, and Harry Lauder was only one of many who paid their dues in the Glasgow 'Bursts' (named after the bursting of bags in which buns were handed out to the audiences at these temperance concerts), organised as counter-attractions to the music halls. One reporter described such a concert of 1886 in Glasgow's working-class Bridgeton as having 'a motley audience, from the old toper, who was "doing" the teetotlar – down to the beardless boy who sported his lass'. In 'A Stormy Night at the Bridgeton Bursts' we read of the 'beardless youths'

> *… who kept clattering to each other the whole night, to the annoyance and disgust of those around them … their expressions consisted of 'Oh Jees', 'He's a Mug', and while a young lady would be doing a 'turn' their remarks were often worse; in vain the chairman begged on them to be quiet, in vain the attendants threatened to expel them … there was also a good many children-in-arms present, and every now and then some infant set up a howl just to let us know it was there ….*

As this suggests, the audiences for these temperance concerts were mixed, but they were mainly the young working class, with a reasonable presence of women. The evidence for the halls points to a similar audience. Looking at reports for three music-hall disasters in Scotland – a fire at the Aberdeen People's Palace of Varieties in 1896, and panics at Springthorpe's Music Hall in Dundee in 1865 and the Star in Glasgow in 1884 – one researcher has found that in all cases the victims were locals from the poor working-class districts in which the theatres were placed.

If there were any middle-class patrons, they were a minority. As David Kennedy's daughter Marjorie Kennedy-Fraser put it, looking back on her touring days in the 1870s, 'Scotland then was austere, and concerts in general and theatres in particular were looked upon askance'. Luckily for the Kennedys, 'our father was always a great favourite of the Scottish clergy ....'. According to J J Bell:

> To the people who regarded the Theatre as placed at the beginning of the road to Hell, the Music Hall was the half-way house; and to many people who occasionally attended the Theatre it was beyond the pale. I daresay that half of the middle-class patrons were there surreptitiously. University students who went to the Gaiety at half-time (and half-price) … were deemed 'fast'. A lady in a Music Hall was unthinkable.

There were, however, distinctions between different halls (the Britannia in Glasgow was favoured by the strong Irish contingent), and increasingly between different sections of the audiences inside the hall. Glasgow detective Alexander Morton gives a good sense of this in a detailed report of the Star Theatre, situated in a densely populated area off the Gallowgate:

> Though the theatre was established in a tenement over a barber's shop, it was constructed internally pretty much after the manner of a theatre. There were stalls and pit on the ground floor, and two galleries stretching from the sides of the stage round the back wall of the house. Its seating capacity was for over 2000 persons. Entrance to the stalls, boxes, and balcony was gained by the principal door in Watson Street and a spacious stairway. Accommodation for the less affluent patrons, as usual, deteriorated in due proportion to their financial worth. Pit and gallery patrons entered by the lesser stair in Watson Lane ….

As for audience behaviour, the Star must have had good reasons for having 25 attendants to deal with any trouble, but it is hard to draw conclusions: one person's dangerous mayhem could be another's good night out. There is little doubt that audiences 'interacted' a good deal, joining together in favourite choruses, and were not slow to express disapproval, with rotten

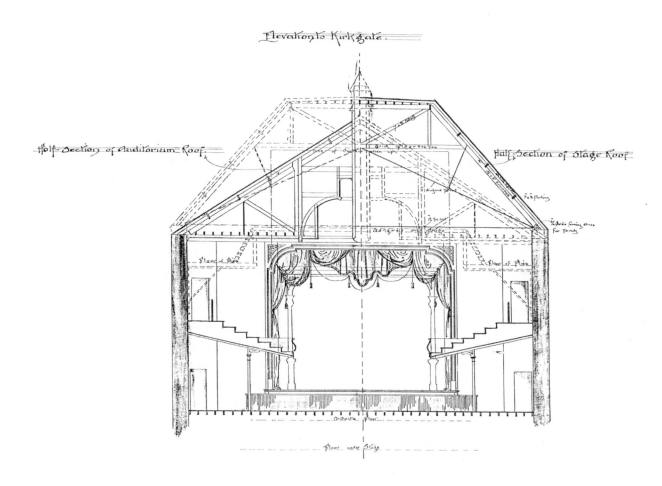

Plan of proposed alterations to Leith Gaiety, 1899 (*see page 24*). (Edinburgh City Archives)

fruit and rivets if necessary. Amateur nights in particular seemed to encourage robust audience participation. A A MacGregor remembered Friday night 'go-as-you please' concerts in Edinburgh's Pringle's Palace in Grove Street and the Operetta House in Chambers Street, as 'the peak of the weeks existence … a night of unmitigated riot' for 'louder and more licentious audiences'. A typical night might have as first turn a young woman singing 'Annie Laurie' with the audience 'joining lustily in the last verse', followed by a navvy dressed in his work clothes, 'cord trousers with straps round the knees; broad leather belt, studded with regimental badges … Kirkcaldy stripe shirt with several patches in it; silk muffler of red magnificence wound round his thick neck …'. He remembered one such performer starting his song before the orchestra was ready, then forgetting the words:

> *Showers of coppers, intermixed with orange peel, then descended on the stage … a youth might slip down a pillar, from the upper gallery to the lower, to aim, from better vantage, a cabbage at the retiring songster. Navvy and cabbage usually reached the wings about the same time …*

In most reports of 'rough houses', however, the near-riots described were due to the non-appearance of a promised pro, and were not necessarily the norm. According to an 1886 report, 'Britannia Music Hall – Minutes of a rough house' in Glasgow music-hall journal *The Professional*, the 'terrific storm of hissing, yelling and howling' which resulted when a favourite clog dancer did not show, was a type of scene 'seldom seen in a music hall'. Neil McFadyen's experience indicates that such scenes may well have been more common in minor venues with less to lose. He recalled one packed Saturday night at the Alhambra in Govan (another converted church) when the band and several artistes did not show up:

> *Those of us who did arrive refused to go on without any music. After waiting some time, the audience began to get definitely out of hand. Some of them climbed on the stage and began shows of their own, all singing different songs. Somebody drew up one of the curtains, the rope broke, and the heavy roller fell down with a bang. Then some of the shipyard workers produced paper bags, filled with rubbish, and these they hurled at the would-be performers till the place was a ghastly mess from flies to footlights. Then, to make matters worse, someone turned out the gas. In the resulting scramble we hid under the stage. When the police arrived – as they frequently did at these shows – our clothes had disappeared. I reached home that night in dancing clogs, frock coat, and red tartan trousers.*

Pros tend to spice up their reminiscences with such 'lively' incidents, when in fact they may not have been typical. But typical or not, unseemly audience behaviour was a subject of great concern for moral crusaders. It was also a problem for theatre managers who wanted to attract the affluent 'respectable' audience and avoid problems with the patchwork of local government committees and panels that issued entertainment licences (usually involving Justices of the Peace and police commissioners). For example, in a minute of the meeting of the Burgh of Dundee Improvement Committee of the Commissioners of Police for 29 August 1881 among notices of compulsory purchases, road-paving and the like, a theatre licence is granted to H D Hicks:

> … to carry on public entertainments, consisting of singing optical illusions, dioramas and dramatic sketches, in his portable theatre in the Old Cattle Market … provided satisfactory certificates are produced by Mr Hicks as to the character of the entertainments … and otherwise conforming with the Statue and Bye-laws ….

Impresarios went to great trouble to reassure these high-minded committees, as in the following 1882 petition from D S McKay to Edinburgh JPs for his St Mary's Hall. Once again we find the rigid division between legitimate and non-legitimate blurred: McKay applies for a license for stage plays, rather than the more usual license that prohibited spoken drama, since at this particular venue stage plays were performed in addition to 'other acts'. He stresses the propriety of the venture and claims that the hall was:

> … built for and used by a society having for its main object the moral, social and intellectual improvement of its members. That amongst other laudable and legitimate means towards the furtherance of their design recourse is to be had to social gatherings, soirees, concerts and dramatic entertainments ….

This kind of language was the result of the often fierce opposition put up by local worthies. In 1875, for example, some influential Glaswegians started a campaign against the local halls, visiting several, in particular Whitebait's, where they were shocked by the sight of the 'Francis Parisian ballet troupe' with a can-can programme, and the 'Sisters Ridgway, the clever duettists and dancers'; young women 'so scantily clothed as to be almost naked dancing upon stages before crowds of men, sitting drinking beer and spirits, and smoking cigars and pipes, whilst men sang songs both blasphemous and filthy …'. A public meeting followed, police reports were commissioned, magistrates were petitioned and eventually Whitebait's alcohol license was refused.

The year 1875 was significant in general, with music-hall legislation that was passed to improve safety measures causing problems for many. William Clark reacted angrily and at length through the pages of the *Dunfermline Journal* (a Clark family business) to criticisms in the pages of the rival *Press* about safety standards. He then rounded on Bailie Dick for daring to comment on the running of the hall 'with a deal of tall talk about the Magistrates, the Sheriff, or the Home Secretary taking cognizance of the matter'. Bailie Dick himself was responsible for disturbances in the hall, Clark implies, by not having enough police officers in attendance to nip trouble in the bud.

It was also the year Harry Moss took the first step in a career that was to help shape the future of the business across the United Kingdom. Moss's father James, diorama proprietor from Ashton-under-Lyne and a favourite at Glasgow's 'Davie Broon's Hall' as 'the fiddling comedian', had taken over the Lorne Music Hall in Greenock in the 1870s. In 1877, aged 25, Moss junior struck out on his own and took over the lease of the Edinburgh Gaiety. In line with a growing trend, he hoped to 'elevate' the stan-

dard of performance. John Wilson MacLaren (who claims to have helped Moss buy a second-hand lock and bar on the very day he took it over) remembered that his efforts did not appeal to many of the old patrons and for weeks the performers sang to half-empty benches:

By dogged determination … a purified atmosphere prevailed at the 'Moss Varieties' …. Mr Moss quickly realised that bumper houses could be brought about only by strengthening what had always been a very mediocre programme. It was a bold step to take, and a daring bid for fortune, but he was confident that, if a London 'star' could be brought to Edinburgh every week, it would satisfy not only the regular patrons but induce many others to patronise his establishment. This innovation was speedily instituted, the result being that, in spite of their scruples, respectable folk at last found their way into the 'Varieties'.

By booking top London acts, Moss kept this more lucrative audience, and in 1880 he took over another theatre in Leith. In 1883 he branched into England, taking over the Sunderland Theatre Royal and in 1884 the New Tyne Concert Hall in Newcastle. By 1890 he had, in conjunction with South Shields showman Richard Thornton, opened the first of his Empires in Newcastle, followed in 1892 by the Edinburgh Empire Palace. These were rapidly followed by the chain of Moss-Thornton Empires across the county, mostly, like the 1897 Glasgow Empire and 1905 Glasgow Coliseum, designed by the prolific theatre architect Frank Matcham.

Attempts at 'improvement' had been made from the start of the music-hall era. The first proprietor of the Scotia ran his hall on temperance lines for a number of years, and claims for the refinement and educational value of programmes were a feature of promotion. In a

Aberdeen Tivoli (*external; for internal picture, see page 24*).

Aberdeen Tivoli (internal detail).
Originally built as Her Majesty's Opera House in 1872 to host plays and
opera, the building was revamped by renowned theatre architect Frank
Matcham in 1897 and again in 1909 when it reopened as the Tivoli,
an opulent de-luxe variety theatre.

this 'improvement' was on a new scale. De-luxe halls were inaugurated, completing an evolution from the glorified pubs of the 1850s to what were in effect theatres, with fixed and segregated seats and refreshments removed into the foyers. This was aimed at satisfying the scruples of 'respectable' audiences.

In addition to new buildings, older theatres were refurbished and expanded, often several times. Metal merchant Frederick R Graham Yooll had a theatre reconstructed out of a Leith Kirkgate church building in 1888 (opened in 1889 by Harry Moss), raised the proscenium (front part of the stage), made space to expand the stage and install dressing rooms by demolishing a nearby tenement in 1899 (re-opened as the Gaiety under R C Buchanan), and in 1913 installed new entrances and exits (see page 19). In the East End of Glasgow a consortium of Glasgow councillors advertised the November 1892 reopening of the People's Palace (a name loaded with improving overtones) in fulsome terms:

… Refined Music Hall Variety Entertainments for the People. The Theatre will be open every evening all the year round, and everything will be produced on a scale and under rules of Management never before attempted in this country, with the determination that no effort will be spared for

second burst of music-hall innovation which took place around the United Kingdom from the late 1880s, largely spearheaded by Moss,

the comfort and convenience of their supporters .... Booked Seats to the working classes For 3d., 6d., or 1s., just the same as the wealthy West-End Merchant books his seat for the opera ....

These enlarged, improved or brand-new theatres were increasingly syndicated into nationwide chains across Britain. In addition to Moss's Empires, the circus Livermore brothers built the Dundee Palace (1893) and Aberdeen Palace (1898) to run in conjunction with Palaces in Sunderland, Bristol and Weymouth. Across the United Kingdom, many of these de-luxe theatres were situated away from the city centres to attract audiences in the growing urban sprawls. In Glasgow the vast Coliseum was built on the south side, and the Tivoli Variety Theatre at Anderston Cross which opened in 1899 was part of a typically modern amusement enclave with Annovazzi's Fish Restaurant, A Moncogni & Co, selling 'Ice Cream and Hot Pies', and two pubs, Rorke's 'Old Anderston Houff' and Cowan's 'Favourite' Bar, all nearby:

When tae the 'Tivoli' ye gang, dinna forget tae ca'
On Hughie Cowan, wha sells a dram tae suit baith
*   great an' sma';*

His whusky's guid, his yill's guid, his brandy's a'
*   three staur,*
There's nae hoose in Glesca can bate the Favourite
*   Baur.*

Music hall had reached its zenith, supporting several opulent theatres that showed top international acts, and numerous small-scale local ventures with more home-grown talent. Within a few years, however, with the advent of cinema, all this would change.

Britannia Theatre, Glasgow, showing rough wooden seating.

George Cruikshank

Cruikshank's illustration of amateurs making-up for a private theatrical
production of 'Macbeth' shows one of many manifestations of the 'kiltie',
in this case in the blurred zone between high and low culture.

FROM HARRY LINN TO HARRY LAUDER

By the 1880s, when teenaged collier Harry Lauder first ventured into the local singing competitions around Hamilton, the role of 'Scotch' comic was well-established and enjoying something of a boom. Lauder was just one in a throng of young workers eager to escape the grind of life in industrial Scotland and try his luck as a Scotch comic.

Forty years earlier the situation was less clear-cut: Scottish comic performers were a mixed group made up of favourite singers of various types of comic Scots songs, Robert Burns reciters and actors lured by greater rewards downmarket. There was no clear-cut stage role. Two Edinburgh examples give an idea of the range of performers. Printer's apprentice Robert Pillans progressed from singing with his workmates in a nearby 'free and easy' in the 1840s to appearing in local pantomimes or as Dandie Dinmont and the like in Walter Scott adapta-

tions during the 1860s and '70s, before, like so many performers, he died young from drink in 1878. He was part music-hall performer, part actor, part local singer. Brass-finisher turned singer James Lumsden's 43-year career began in the 1850s. As his *Scotsman* obituary recollected, he went on to specialise in

> … *humorous Scottish songs. He also gave sketches of Scottish character, such as Tam o' Shanter and Soutar Johnnie … for twenty-five years in succession Mr. Lumsden was asked by the Aberdeen Temperance Society to provide their musical festival on new year's night …. The Burns festival in the Music Hall Edinburgh was another event with which his name was associated for many years.*

By the 1880s, however, a distinct genre of Scottish performers had developed, part of a

Rob Roy from an 1881 burlesque production entitled 'Robbing Roy' at the Glasgow Royalty – visually there was little to differentiate the various stage kilties. (*Quiz*)

wider trend for regional stereotypes in music hall across Britain, especially 'Cockney' singers (two notable examples of which, W G Ross and Arthur Lloyd, had come down from Scotland). James Houston acknowledged this shift in his 1889 Autobiography of James Houston, *Scotch Comedian*, talking of a 'great Scotch Comic singer' of his youth, continuing 'little did I think, after an interval of forty years, I should appear in my native city a full-blown Scotch Comedian …'. Singers of Scotch comic songs had become 'Scotch Comics'.

These more professionalised performers assembled their repertoire from many sources: the various traditions of polite and not so polite Scottish song (of which more in the chapter on 'Scottish Song and Musical Acts', page 73), and the stage-Scot of conventional drama (given such massive exposure in innumerable stage adaptations of Walter Scott novels). Finally, we might mention the ornate and ubiquitous Scot of Victorian military spectacle.

Much of this Caledoniana was well recycled in the cultural marketplace across the United Kingdom. The tartan-clad 'kiltie' had long dominated popular imagination, appearing across the entertainment spectrum north and south of the Border: displaced Highlanders played on the image as urban buskers; a puppet Scotsman danced the Highland fling alongside an Italian scaramouch, hornpiping sailor and Indian juggler in a London street puppet theatre of the 1850s; a troupe of be-tartaned stilt-walkers cross the pages of Charles Dickens' *The Old Curiosity Shop*, and the Royal City of London Theatre offered (among innumerable other attractions, including 'celebrated dogs Hector and Bruin') on the following Wednesday, 1 February 1843

> *… Double Highland fling, Mdle Cushnie and Sig. Milano – Dancing Scotchmen – Fiddling Scotchmen – Sleeping Scotchmen – the Old Bailey and the New Bailey – Bag and other wind instruments – Munificent presentation of real Scotch fiddle by Old Scratch ….*

For non-Scottish audiences the 'kiltie' stood for Scots in general. For the Lowland urban majority in Scotland, Highlanders had been 'ethnic outsiders' since before the Reformation, but the stereotype gained new life with the influx of cleared Highlanders to city slums, and it became a staple of the popular stage, and a useful vehicle to explore uncertainties about modern city life.

Most Scots comics had a stock of 'characters' ranging from sentimentally bucolic to robustly urban. This somewhat overlapped a torrent of vernacular writing in the regional popular periodicals and many wrote for both the popular stage and popular press. Printer James Smith produced vernacular periodical prose, poems of every hue, and songs and sketches for his own performances as well as for the likes of James Houston and James Lumsden.

A typical result of all this updating and reworking was a performer like Harry Linn, at his peak in the 1870s and '80s. His *Glasgow Evening Times* obituary remembered him thus:

> *… anyone who knows the lives and surroundings of our younger Clyde mechanics can testify that, in spending their 3d or 6d one or two evenings in the fortnight, they might, in a moral sense, go farther and fare worse …. Harry Linn was peculiarly fitted to please an audience of this class. He could not sing, but what of that? … his voice, if somewhat reedy, was strong enough to fill the hall. His songs were written by himself, but were never known to have any claim to literary merit …. These songs, however, portrayed the everyday types of humanity with which his audiences were familiar, tinctured with a strong colouring of Stockwell Street and Trongate humour ….*

Any apparent realism in Linn's act, however, depended on careful blending of ingredients with performers adopting the exaggerated conventions of mainstream music hall to

William Lannagan, one of the first generation of Scotch comics, striking a pose in character for 'The Lads that were Reared Amang the Heather'.

produce the Scottish equivalents of the bill-topping comics of the national circuit. Glasgow bricklayer WH Lannagan, for example, developed a successful career as 'The Scottish Lion Comedian' in imitation of the bewhiskered champagne-drinking swell character, the best known of which was George Leybourne, or 'Champagne Charlie'.

Scots comediennes worked a similar repertoire to nationally popular comediennes like Jenny Hill and Bessie Bellwood (who topped a bill at the Glasgow Gaiety in September 1894, with a young Harry Lauder appearing nearer the bottom). Glasgow's Marie Loftus was a pantomime favourite, and Bessie Arthur appeared across Scotland in the 1890s with sentimental songs like 'Dinna quarrel ma bairnies', 'The banks o the Clyde', or wife's lament 'The fitba victim':

I've got the very worst man that a woman ever had
Search the world frae end to end, ye'll no find yin
sae bad
For since he's jined a fitba' club my life's no' worth a
straw,
Maist every nicht he plays the game, an' its me
that is the ba'.

Of Alice Brookes who appeared in songs and sketches with her partner Fanny Wright, an 1889 Grand Theatre Glasgow pantomime reviewer tells us that 'she works hard, acts with great spirit and sings and dances with all her well-known cleverness ...'. Her gossip-song 'Ye micht ha'e kept that tae yersel', is a Scottish revamping of a music-hall staple:

> We do not like neebor's tae clash oor affairs,
> Ye micht ha'e kept that tae yersel';
> We're no in the habit o' meddlin' wi' theirs,
> Ye micht ha'e kept that tae yersel'.
> Inquisitive gossips, wi' tongues unco slack,
> Delight tae tell stories ahint a freen's back;
> But we never bother wi' that kind o' crack.
> Ye micht ha'e kept that tae yersel'.

The Scotch comics' repertoire was something of a mixed bag. A type of 'newsy' song about specific events, much in the old street ballad tradition, was to be found as late as J H Redmonde's 'topical' song of 1900 for Willie Frame:

> I ha'e a few bit words tae say
> Aboot the topics o' the day,
> Just in a simple kin o' way,
> That occurred tae me this morning,
> Hey! Colquhoun, are you walking yet

> On the treadmill, in your moleskin suit?
> Ye thocht ye were fly, but ye got bit
> Sweet five year, in the morning.

> Across the sea there wis a race
> That for the Yankee Cup took place,
> When the Shamrock yacht went out tae pace
> The Columbia in the morning,
> Tammy Lipton, man, oh dinna grieve
> Altho' the cup ye had tae leave ... &c

Occasionally this topicality might take a more overtly political position, as in prolific writer Tom McAusland's 1895 song 'The Clyde lock out':

> Why did the maisters lock them oot?
>   Why turn awa' the man?
> They had nae grievance o' their ain, nae grievance
>   that I ken,
> The wheels wir rinnin' smoother than they've din
>   for years gane past,
> Then why mak' their men suffer for thir tyrants in
>   Belfast.
> The maisters think that workin' men in 'Union'
>   shouldna be,
> An' yet they're sworn in yin thirsel's which looks
>   gey queer tae me.

> ... Instead o' votin for sich men, I'd fling them in
>   the tide,

*It's men like thae hae brocht aboot this lock oot on
the Clyde.*

In general, however, re-workings of music-hall standards seem to have been most common, as in the songs about novelties, fads and crazes, like Neil MacFadyen's 'Cycling Geordie' or John Alexander's 'The Scots American Herbalist'. Audience experience was reflected in more conservative, often nostalgic or sentimental songs about the humours of married, family or working life strumming on perennial and communal themes. Typically in this hybrid format there would be a humorous play of the mundane and the metropolitan. Harry Linn's 'Jimmy, Tak' Your Sunday Claes Aff', can stand for many hundreds of such 'bi-lingual' songs with its faddish 'straight' music-hall verse and contrasting chorus:

I'm what they call a weekly swell, I've got a suit,
*   you see,*
And all the neighbours say this suit just fits me to
*   a T:*
Only once a week I am allowed to have them on,
'Cause every Monday morning they have to go to
*   pawn,*
And every Sunday afternoon, when sitting down
*   to tea,*
My wife she winks, then she blinks, and then she
*   says to me –*

Jimmy, tak' your Sunday claes aff, mind you brush
*   them well,*
Only once a week you can afford to be a swell;
Roll them up in a table cloth, give them to the girl,
She'll take them to your 'Uncle' in the morning.

It's only forty years ago since first this suit was made
But the tailors forty years ago were stunners at their
*   trade;*
For twenty years, one day a week, I've worn it
*   myself,*
And six days out of every week it has been upon
*   the 'shelf' … [and so on]*

Such songs were not tied to a specific place (which suited the touring performer) and they appealed to working and lower middle-class audiences in general by reflecting uncontroversial values like thrift, dislike of ostentation or appearing different.

Finding the right mix of ingredients which would 'click' with an audience was the job of the army of largely working-class *littérateurs* who kept the song-sheets full with literally thousands of songs. Glasgow and the west of Scotland seems to have been something of a song-writing centre for the United Kingdom in general, supporting two long-running song magazines, Barr's *Professional* and the *Amateur*, carrying a mixture of trade gossip and what must be tens of thousands of songs over the decades. The contributors to these rags were adept across the music-hall spectrum, writing not only Scottish material but also Irish songs, emigrant songs, patriotic songs, Dixie songs emulating those made popular by American 'Minstrel' shows, patter songs, parodies of Scotch songs (and of all the other types), masher songs about fashionable young men, football songs, humorous readings and 'stump speeches'. Perhaps the most prolific was the 'Parody King' James Curran, originally from Ireland, who by 1890, when he made a performing debut in the Britannia Music Hall Glasgow, is claimed to have written around 1200 songs and parodies.

Pros depended on these writers, just as writers hoped to write for the best performers. Harry Lauder was already enough of a name by 1894 for Tom Glen, author of some of his earliest successes, to advertise himself as 'Author and composer to the Elite of the Music Hall profession. Author of Harry Lauder's "Miner", "Tooralada", &c.; also, R.C. M'Gill's "Scotchmen and Irishmen". Terms moderate and nothing sold twice'. However, relationships were often strained. Performers would buy sole rights to songs and played down the role of the writers. As Sandy Melville, one of Lauder's writers, complained in 1903:

'Saftest o' the Family' was a Lauder reworking of a well-established type, and one of his most popular sketches. Rather like Chaplin's 'little man' it appealed to submerged anxieties about coping in rapidly changing modern industrial society.

… he says 'My first successful song was "The Bonnie Wee Man",' but he never let dab that all he stumped up for that song was the magnificent sum of 3s! Swell houses for the singers and poor-houses for the writers! James Curran, my old pal, made fortunes for a lot of self-styled comedians, and what did they do? Nothing!

For his part in one of his biographies, Lauder recalled 'Poor Sandy Melville' as a sad drunk, happy to sell the odd item as he wasted away in an east-end pub. The reality was unsentimental. Pros talked down and writers talked up their contribution, and in any case they were happy to plagiarise and sell the same song many times over. As another writer for Lauder, Neil McFadyen, reveals:

The moment any comedian produces a new idea it is copied by dozens of others …. I have written as many as four songs in a day at prices from five shillings each …. there used to be the constant trouble of some song-writers selling the same song over and over again, till a host of comedians found they had all bought the same song.

There was little difference between outright theft or slight adaptation from a stock of comic formulae. Most of Lauder's 'characters' had antecedents: his gormless 'saftest o' the family'

was in a long line of daft gowk characters, and 'Sandy saft a wee', for example, was a speciality of J C MacDonald, one of his early mentors.

Despite all the efforts of Scotch comics and their writers, however, audiences paid more to see 'national' stars who topped the bills in the larger venues. Scotch comics were often found further down the bills, and at works soirées and suchlike; or, as we have seen, they became impresarios as well as performers, not always with much success. Harry Linn took over the lease of a Greenock hall from James Moss, hoping to cash in on his reputation. Greenock folk were not impressed and he had to beg a local councillor to come and endorse his failing enterprise.

More successful was R C McGill, who gave Lauder an early break in 1886. Working in the Govan shipyards, he won medals in singing competitions and went professional, specialising in Scotch character songs such as 'A shilling in your pocket is the best freen' ye ha'e'. His career was based largely on self-organised 'Saturday evening concerts' in Leith and other non-music hall appearances. Willie Frame was one of the most successful showman-comedians, though not as unique as he suggests in his 1907 autobiography (a showbusiness puff, almost certainly written in response to Lauder's success). He made his first public appearance in Glasgow in

1867 and was still performing in the 1920s. He ran his own touring concert parties, and in 1886, the same year as Linn's venture, took on an 18-month lease of the well-established Glasgow venue 'Davie Broon's', renaming it 'Frame's Royal Music Hall'. He only gave it up due to the demands of his touring. By 1894 he was described by Glasgow periodical *Quiz* as 'one of the best known of the present-day men in Scotland'.

Frame made something of a breakthrough to 'respectability' with regular appearances in the posher Glasgow and Edinburgh pantomimes and ultimately became a Justice of the Peace. This 'respectability' had largely eluded the first generation of Scotch comics, but by the 1880s and '90s, as music hall in general became more 'respectable', those who kept carbolically clean began to reach a wider audience. Frame's success depended on this and *Quiz* noted his 'exceeding refinement … with that purity … which permeates his entire entertainment'. For his part, Lauder's biographies reveal an almost pathological concern for propriety.

As well as trying to widen their local audience many Scottish comedians, including Frame, had a pitch at national and international success. James Houston had gone down to London in 1862, but as he remarked 'I did not make a big hit – for the audience did not

W F Frame in a typical working-man role from the 1890s and of a type which, alongside the Kiltie, remained a staple of the Scotch comic repertoire well into the variety era. (*Quiz*)

understand me very well' and he ended up singing 'more English' songs. Willie Frame's 1889 London debut faltered due to the language barrier, though he had more luck following in the footsteps of several predecessors like James Lumsden and Jack Lorimer (father of Max Wall) touring the ex-patriate Scottish communities of North America in 1898. It was Lauder who made the real break to the big-time.

By 1900 he was having some success in northern England with the sort of Hibernian character act popular with the Irish in Glasgow. But as he recalled in his autobiography, he fancied 'a cut at the metropolitan stage'. He had seen Dan Leno and other London stars at the Glasgow Empire and decided that 'if Dan Leno can get a hundred pounds a week for singing London songs in Glasgow, I can get at least twenty for singing Scotch comic songs in London'. He modified his act to suit the mass market of the big circuits, ironing out anything too local or idiomatic: 'I decided that if ever I got a footing in England I would not use words or idioms which would only befog my audience. I would sing my songs in English, I determined, *but with a Scottish accent.*' Earlier 'trashy' songs were either abandoned or reworked, often, as his song credits show, with the help of top southern writers and composers.

Two versions of his breakthrough song 'Call again, Calligan' show the change. Both share the same story of working-class life; the singer has his clothes made by Calligan and pays weekly until work falls off and he finds that he cannot pay, has a dispute with the tailor, and tells him to 'call again', offering to return the debated trousers. The first version in 1897 ends with a fist-fight – 'he drew his fist and knocked my front teeth slack' – and is typical of the repertoire that went down well with 'rough-houses' in the Glasgow halls. This is like another of Lauder's early songs about a pavement brawl over a girl, Sandy Melville's 'Hauns aff – that belangs tae me':

> *Hauns aff – that belangs tae me*
> *Then I got a punch upon the e'e,*
> *Leave her alane, so I did you see,*
> *Hauns aff – for she belangs tae me.*

By 1905, however, matters were more genteel. In the reworked Calligan song there is nothing more heated than 'I really thought our words would come to blows'. There would be no fisti-cuffs in the world of 'Roamin in the gloamin'.

Lauder had taken his time to hone his act. In a 1903 interview with the *Glasgow Weekly News* he says:

1906 sheet music cover. Lauder plays the absurdly stingy Scot,
wearing a kilt so that his wife cannot search his trouser pockets for money,
in a song calculated for mass, rather than local, appeal with
its 'battle of the sexes' theme. This kiltie is a mild hybrid compared
with the excesses often perpetrated in the genre.

I had my e'e on London, but I wanted a bit o' experience afore I tackled that job, so I did the Empires in the provinces. When I was offered a turn in London I was just a wee bit feart I didna ken ma business weel eneuch, and I hung aff for near three years. I didna lose onything by that.

By the time Lauder made his breakthrough the local Scotch comic boom had peaked, with the number of songs written especially for them in the song magazines falling off through the 1890s. In any case they had never surpassed the popularity of stars of the national circuit. For a middle-class patron like J J Bell, Scotland had nothing to compare with coster singers Gus Elen and Albert Chevalier:

The 'Scotch Comic' eschewed sweetness and light. If he introduced sentiment, it was of the greasy, spurious sort. For his comicality he depended too often on the sordid aspects of life. Without drink and domestic misery he would have had little to sing about …. It was then, I suppose, a sort of convention that Scottish comedians should present Scottish life at its lowest, and Scotland really owes something to its laughter-makers of a later day, who had the genius and courage to smash the convention.

The likes of Willie Frame and J C MacDonald may have widened their audience, but Harry Lauder must take the credit for fully reinventing the Scotch Comic masque and revitalising the careers of scores of former local comics as Lauder imitators. Aberdeen hairdresser Donald MacDougall hung up his scissors and was by the early 1900s working the small-time local trades concert circuit as 'Albert Windsor – Aberdeen's leading characteristic comedian'. But following a 1908 pantomime breakthrough he moved south to Birkenhead, ditched his Doric material and jumped on the Lauder bandwagon, being reviewed as 'another addition to the long list of Scotch Comedians'. In 1909 he was engaged to join a two-year tour of South Africa with the 'Musical Madcaps', billed as 'Scotland's Second Harry Lauder', enjoying such success in this role that he emigrated to continue his career.

Inevitably, the proliferation of the Lauder-esque invited parody, as in several songs that were recorded by Australian Billy Williams (see next page):

THE
HIGHLANDMAN'S TOAST
WORDS & MUSIC BY
HARRY LINN

POPULAR SONGS BY THE SAME COMPOSER

THE HIGHLANDMANS TOAST 3/- | THE GRASS WILL GROW AGAIN 3/-
I LOVE THE BONNIE LASSES 3/- | NORAH MAGEE 3/-
BONNIE JEANIE DEANS 3/- | THE AULD PAIR O' TAWSE 3/-

Ent. Sta. Hall.   Price 3/-

Glasgow.

Like many comedians, Harry Linn (see earlier) tried to present a respectable 'concert platform' image. Though he lists a number of his other straight compositions, he was most associated with his song 'Jock McGraw the fattest man in the forty-twa'.

Since my old woman went to Scotland for
      her holiday
She's got Scotland on the brain,
She's driving me insane.

She used to give me eggs and bacon for my
      breakfast once,
I've been eating nothing else but porridge now
      for months.

[Chorus: to 'Scottified' melody]

She does like a little bit of Scotch ye ken,
She does like a little bit of Scotch.
In the middle of the night she begins to sing,
Jumps out of bed and does the highland fling.
She's christened me Sandy, her ways she'll
      have to watch.
Its a braw bricht moonlicht nicht the nicht.
She does like a little bit of Scotch!
Och aye!

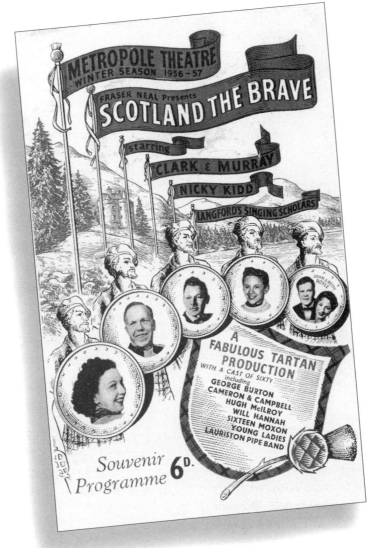

One of a run of 'Scottish' winter shows produced by Fraser Neal at
the Glasgow Metropole theatre. (Archie Foley)

VARIETY DAYS

The 1914-18 War put a brake on wholesale development in showbusiness, but by the early 1920s 'bookings were plentiful with few acts out of work', according to English comedian Bud Flanagan who played many Scottish dates. Over the next two decades, despite years of economic depression, the entertainment industry in general expanded rapidly.

French-polisher George Clarkson teamed up with four other Motherwell lads, and as 'The Five Jocks' filled his date book in the early '20s playing a multitude of venues in the industrial heart of Scotland and the north of England. For 1919 we have the Victoria Kilsyth, Empire Clydebank, the Pavilion Ayr, Lyceum Govan, Olympia Dunfermline, Pavilion Wishaw, Empire Cowdenbeath, Empire Motherwell, Olympia Bridgeton and Grand Falkirk. The list goes on – every little town had its Empire, Olympia, Palace or Pavilion. Clarkson claimed that at this time there were some 60 halls within easy reach of Motherwell and playing them in turn could take up to two years. According to dancer May Moxon, there were 20 possible venues to play in Glasgow alone.

THE PAVILION. MOSSEND.

One of many cine-variety venues built across central Scotland early in the century, the 850-seat Mossend Pavilion opened in December 1912 with a bill of films and variety artistes: Daisy and Dots, The Mammons with 'pawky American humour' and Professor Markie 'whose rendering of the opera "William Tell" on 25 ordinary bottles is unique in the variety world'.

However, the business was changing as always. Going to the variety theatre was a weekly ritual for many families, with many having the same seats booked season after season; but audiences were being lured away by the cinemas, the dancing craze, and to a lesser extent, from 1923, the growth of home-based entertainment in the form of radio. The 1916-25 artists' salary book for the Coliseum Theatre, Glasgow (built just a few years earlier) vividly illustrates the changing fortunes of the business.

For January 1917 the expenses were £300 per week for a 'Robinson Crusoe' pantomime, £210 for top star Fred Kitchen, and £2. 10s. for the bioscope show: a relatively modest total of £512. 10s. with a similar story repeated for the following two years' winter shows (starring Glasgow favourite George Formby senior). During the rest of the year, top British and international stars were being paid £100 or more weekly, with Marie Lloyd appearing in December 1920 for a week at £338. 5s., and the pantomime expenses were £1174.

Business was good in the immediate post-war boom. Then decline set in. Cheaper bills with more local talent appeared, more of the packaged revue shows that could be booked for £200 or less, and from 1923 an increasing proportion of the far cheaper option – films. By 1929 this enormous theatre was completely converted to film.

Theatres showed films as part of a variety bill from the start of the century and, in the years leading up to World War I, showbusinessmen increasingly turned to cinema or cine-variety. W 'Prince' Bendon, who had established a reputation as a ventriloquist in concert parties with Lauder and Frame amongst others, and as a exhibition cyclist conquering steep hills and thoroughfares wherever he could find them, was also a cinema pioneer. He introduced 'Bendon's Bioscope' into concert programmes, having travelled down to assess the possibilities as soon as he heard of their advent in London. He is reputed to have been the first film renter in Glasgow.

A spate of dedicated cine-variety venues were built, particularly across the Central Belt. E H Bostock of the famous circus family had a network of Scottish showbusiness interests in circus, menageries, music hall, dancing, roller-skating and wrestling. By 1914 he had a group of venues that included the multi-purpose Hamilton's Hippodrome and Victoria Hall, the Rink Picture Palace, and Paisley Hippodrome. One of the most active figures of the early years of the century, former elocution teacher and theatre manager, R C Buchanan, established a chain of variety theatres. Being quick to spot the potential of cinema, he built a number of pioneer picture houses across the Central Belt.

By 1917, when circus clown Henry Whiteley played a Scottish tour, it was made up entirely of cine-variety. As he notes in his autobiography:

… cine variety was going very strong. Fred Collins agency just started with booking at Electric Falkirk, MacQueens Agency, MacFarlane Agency, Kenyons Agency, Galt Agency etc .… Green Tour Galashiels, Kilburnie, Penicuik, Linlithgow, Dunbar, Peebles, also … several small halls in Glasgow, Ayr etc .…

Most of the engagements listed in George Clarkson's date book for 1919 and the early '20s were in cine-variety. Many were purpose-built – like one of Flanagan's first Scottish dates, the Olympia Bridgeton, which was equipped for cinema from its 1911 opening; or the Empire Electric Theatre in Clarkson's home town, which opened to such good business in 1911 that by the end of the year, as the *Motherwell Times* noted, it was in need of enlargement: 'At every performance this week hundreds have been turned away unable to gain admission' for a bill that included a film about Irish patriot Rory O'More, singer and whistler Jessie Star, the Randles in a comedy sketch, and xylophone experts The Five Veronas. However, a growing number of dates were in music halls given over to cinema, with a couple of variety turns on the bill. Throughout the 1920s

Opened as a variety theatre in 1909 the King's Theatre, Dundee also hosted musicals, plays, opera, ballet and ice spectaculars before converting to cinema in 1928, and sharing the fate of many not-long-built variety theatres in the 1920s and '30s. (Scottish Life Archive)

The Armadale Empire Palace was a 500-seat cine-variety venue converted in 1910 from an existing billiard hall and skating rink by Irish showman Micky Burns. Though rather humble-looking it was no doubt an escape to comparative comfort for its audience. (Scottish Life Archive)

many of the large theatres built only ten or 20 years earlier shared the fate of the Coliseum.

In both cases, while cine-variety was a welcome source of work, it was far from ideal for pros. Flanagan recalled a tour organised by agent Fred Collins which started at Wick:

When I saw the theatre I was dumbfounded; no scenery, just a cinema backcloth; no stage but a platform with benches in the stalls. Wick was a fishing place, neither a village nor a town. The show was only once nightly and, as we made our entrance, a meat pie narrowly missed my head and hit the cinema screen. As the gravy ran down the sheet, I gaped at the audience. They couldn't have known whether we were good or bad as we hadn't uttered a word, but they were all laughing, and even the 'orchestra' (a piano) was doubled up.

The final venue of this Scottish tour was the Pavilion Stockbridge, a 2000-seater built in 1901, and by 1920 devoted to film: 'Like Wick, there was a platform, no stage, and a cinema sheet behind ....'

The style of entertainment was also changing in response to the cinema challenge. As at the Glasgow Coliseum, revues (touring companies of variety artistes with a themed show of loosely-linked comedy sketches, novelty and instrumental acts, and sentimental song-scenes using all the cast) were, from the turn of the century, replacing the older music-hall bills of individually booked artistes appearing in their own spot, one after the other. By the 1920s revues were becoming the norm. As George Clarkson's Five Jocks moved up the professional ladder, they increasingly played week after week in different theatres, two shows a night. Their first was 'Stunners' which, after a fortnight's holiday and a week's rehearsal, was on the road from February 1923 until March 1924 (followed by 'Grumbles' of 1924-25). The press notice for an English appearance gives a good idea of this all-Scottish show:

The entertainment is in programme form, comprising fifteen numbers in all, and each of them finds its own particular admirers in the audience. Our Scotch visitors will welcome the appearance of Mr. George Clarkson in some fine dancing scenas, and it is doubtful if a more accomplished artist in this line has been seen here for a long time. In the number, 'Boys Together', Mr. Clarkson, made up as a feeble old man, suddenly breaks out into a lightning dance turn, and secured a rapturous applause. 'Leisure moments at Sea' is an hilarious number, and gave Mr. Clarkson another chance to show his skill in a whirlwind hornpipe. Mr. Bernard Ash, a violinist of considerable ability, is constantly before the audience with some charming solos, and

On stage at the Greenock Empire, September 1945.
Comedian Jimmy Nicol is in the centre of the middle row, 'Moxon Girls' are at the front,
and in the back row the local torpedo factory pipe band.

in a drawing room scene plays obbligatos to the
vocal numbers. Miss May Wills and Miss Jose
Donelli sang as a duet the famous 'Caller Herrin'
song in costume, and were warmly applauded.
An Australian trio burlesque caused abundance
of laughter, and the musical ensembles were well
received ....

'Grumbles' was an all-Scottish revue of a type
of that, with modifications, continued until the
end of the variety theatre era, notably in a series
of winter shows in the 1940s and '50s at the
Metropole in Glasgow, produced by Fraser Neal,

perhaps best known in the television age in the
form of 'The White Heather Club'.

Apart from this type of show Scottish companies and performers, like their English counterparts, increasingly adopted a style of quick-fire
variety owing much to American vaudeville,
incorporating the latest song, dance and musical
turns, and slick cross-patter sketches alongside
more familiar favourites, with performers
appearing in various different guises throughout
a show. In 'Grumbles', George doubled as
comedian, singer, dancer – an all-round performer with a trademark character sketch as a

To May The Logan Family

Jim *May* *Jack* *Buddy.*

The Logan family. Jack Short and May Dalziel ('Pa' and 'Ma' Logan) had
worked as a double-act since the 1920s, before appearing with
the Logan family. In 1947 they started a run of Logan family shows at the
Metropole Glasgow, described by one theatre journalist as 'part of Glasgow's way of life'.

ship's stoker dancing the hornpipe. This doubling enabled full shows to be spun from a smaller number of performers, an important consideration for cost-conscious promoters sometimes taken to extremes, with dancers from the chorus line being recruited, members of the orchestra, or even, as Bill McLenaghan told me, the comedian's chauffeur:

I used to get wee bit parts … what they called 'spoke money'; he was gettin' a sketch on, and he wanted to put a character in, he'd say 'you go in Bill', and I made about a fiver a week. Well, my wages were about six fifty, and that was good wages. Miners were only getting four fifty … just after the war.

Most Scottish producers and comedians came to specialise in these types of shows. In the case of Jack Short and May Dalziel, the whole family was involved as 'The Logan family' in shows across Scotland and Ireland.

Until the advent of the 'talkies' in 1928, live theatre with sound and spectacle had some chance of competing with cinema. Thereafter, and for the next three decades, the business gradually contracted. The sometimes feverish pace of venues changing ownership or management slowed, and as the numbers of theatres diminished across the United Kingdom the clear-cut hierarchy of 'number one, two and three' theatres became relatively fixed until the end of the variety era. The system was based not on the size of theatres, but on profitability. At the top were the few city centre theatres able to book the best international acts which guaranteed full houses. In Scotland, as elsewhere, these included the Moss Empire Theatres and the Howard and Wyndham Theatres, such as the King's Theatres, in Glasgow and Edinburgh.

The Moss Empires, being part of a national circuit, were able to attract bill-topping stars well known from cinema, radio and then television, perhaps including one or two top Scottish acts elsewhere on the bill for good measure. Getting a Moss Empires' contract was a holy grail for pros, meaning weeks of work as they moved from one city to the next on the circuit. For their part the Moss Empires kept an air of exclusivity by stipulating that contracted acts must not play in any other venues. This recipe managed to keep year round business until after World War II, still using the old formula of turns one after another.

Howard and Wyndham specialised in 'production variety shows' (which many considered were not variety at all, but more like light musicals) and, as we shall see later, lavish pantomimes. By the early 1930s city-centre summer business was often so slack that many theatres like the two King's would close. Then in 1933 they tried out summer seasons modelled after the success of the coastal shows which were proving so popular, but with altogether more elaborate staging under top producer Julian Wylie. These reasonably priced 'Half-past Eight' shows were a hit, particularly those starring comedian Dave Willis, then at the top of the profession, and by the 1940s were running for more than 20 weeks, the record being 31 weeks in the 1942 Glasgow show.

A step down from these well-backed venues were the number twos, perhaps smaller, with fewer expensive acts on the bills, and hosting more packaged touring shows, though still yielding good business without too much slack. By the mid 1930s these were virtually synony-

Proprietors Stagecraft Ltd.   Manager Dan Campbell

NEXT WEEK   MONDAY 24th OCTOBER, 1955

MARCHING THRO' THE HEATHER
JOHNNY VICTORY

HECTOR NICOL,   BETTY NOLAN,   DESMOND CARROLL,
BETTY BRIGHT,   LINDSAY DOLAN,   MOXON LADIES,
LORANE and GAYE,   NORMAN TEAL and ROY CASTLE,
PHIL KELLY,   MATT SOUTAR,   ISOBEL MOFFAT,

The Show Devised and Produced by
JOHNNY VICTORY and DESMOND CARROLL

Box Office open 10 a.m. to 9 p.m.   Phone FOU 5151

PUPS, POODLES and PIERRE

Produced by Desmond Carroll   and Starring
JOHNNY VICTORY

1. Song Dance and Laughter   Cast includes Desmond Carroll,
   Betty Bright, Hector Nicol, Betty Nolan, Lindsay Dolan,
   Phil Kelly, Castle & Teal, Lorraine and Gaye, Isobel Moffat,
   Ronnie Coburn, The Victory Belles, and re-introducing
   JOHNNY VICTORY
   Johnny and Hector
2. Smile Awhile   Matt Soutar
3. B.B.C. Accordianist   and the Victory Belles
4. On the Town   with Desmond, Betty, Lindsay, Mary, Roy, Doris,
   Johnny, Betty, Hector, Betty Bright,
   with Johnny and the entire Company
5. Husbands and Wives   Phil Kelly
6. Sweethearts   Lorraine and Gaye
7. Mr Personality   Isobel Moffat
8. Glamour Girls   Johhny, Hector, Ronnie, Betty and Oesmond
9. Sales Talk   Desmond, Betty, Lindsay and
10. Sweetness in Song   the Victory Belles
11. Dancing in Cowboy Style   Johnny, Hector, Betty and company
    Betty Nolan,
12. Pierres Honeymoon   Norman Teale and Roy Castle
13. The Mighty Atom   Johnny Victory
14. Musical Express
15. Scotlands Son of Fun   with the entire company and Johnny
16. World Belief

Wardrobe by Wm. Mutrie of Edinburgh   Scenery by Sam Oxley
Dance routines by Carroll and Bright

Programme for the Edinburgh Palladium showing the standard weekly change of fare — 'Scottish' and 'French' were two of the numerous themes ('Irish', 'Cowboy', 'Gypsy', and so on) on which producers routinely drew.

mous with the chain of theatres built up by the Collins family who, from the early 1920s until after World War II, were arguably the premier Scottish agency.

James Alfred Nelson started his show-business career in the 1890s performing and song-writing, and falling back on his trade as a master painter when times were lean until after the Boer War, when he made headway as a Scotch comic. He changed his name to Fred Collins and thrived in the growing seaside business as a performer and, increasingly, an impresario and agent. The Collins Variety Agency grew, setting up offices at 115 Renfield Street in the heart of Scottish showbusiness. Together with son Horace, they spotted and groomed many of the top Scottish stars of the 1920s and '30s, often signing them to 16-year option contracts. During the 1930s they began to take control of a circuit of theatres, taking the lease of the Theatre Royal in Edinburgh and acquiring major shareholdings in the Tivoli Aberdeen, Palace Dundee, Pavilion Glasgow, and, as an English outpost to lure performers from down south, the Shakespeare in Liverpool.

While the Collins agency had the top Scottish performers, and a grip on the number twos, for sheer volume of business the principal agency was Galts, situated round the corner from Collins at 13 Sauchiehall Street. The agency had been started at the end of the nineteenth century by James Galt, booking turns in and around Hamilton. By the 1930s, under William Galt (a seldom-seen personage, most artistes getting no further than a celebrated hatch from where the well-remembered Nellie Sutherland dispensed or withheld work), they supplied acts and complete shows throughout Scotland, with a circuit including the Paisley Theatre, Hamilton Hippodrome, the New Century Theatre in Motherwell and the Stirling Alhambra, and controlling much of the business at the 'number threes'.

These were the smaller theatres in less lucrative neighbourhoods, which often presented more homely Scottish or Irish fare – family-owned like the Greenock Empire and Edinburgh Palladium or, from the 1940s and '50s, part of the network of theatres under the management of impresario GB Bowie, including the Falkirk Roxy and Motherwell Empire. Galts also booked out much of the talent for the one area of the business which really boomed in the inter-war years – at the seaside.

Portobello Pier *circa* 1900, two views. By the time the famous pier was
built in 1871, holidaymaking and entertainment were well-established in
Portobello. Bathing machines were advertised for hire in 1795 and
Ord's Circus arrived in the late 1790s. The pier was two-thirds of a
mile long and lasted until 1917, by which time there was
the Tower Pavilion and Marine Gardens complex to keep the crowds happy.

AT THE SEASIDE

In 1871 when a group of local businessmen built Portobello pier, there was a variety pavilion on the end with two shows daily. Tourism had been expanding from the middle of the nineteenth century as the railways opened up seaside resorts to middle-class and then to working-class city dwellers able to afford a few days holiday by the seaside. Resorts along the Clyde and Ayrshire coast, and to a lesser extent on the east coast, experienced continuous growth in the numbers of tourists visiting. Where the crowds flocked, entertainers followed.

James Houston describes a typical engagement at Purvis' Gardens in Dunoon in July 1869, when he was engaged by a Mr D Gerletti (superintendent with Mrs Baylis of the Glasgow Scotia Music Hall). Gerletti was giving a series of well-patronised Saturday afternoon open-air concerts, finishing up with a grand display of fireworks:

We had a small platform with retiring rooms erected on the lawn. After the company had each given a song, the ladies and gentlemen had a dance on the green, and with the fireworks skillfully managed by Mr. Gerletti, the entertainment was very pleasant and very successful.

According to Willie Frame, who worked there as comic singer and master of ceremonies, the price of admission to gardens and promenade was sixpence, which entitled one to take part in the dancing on the green and gave entrance to the open-air concert and fireworks after nightfall. It was 'a big sixpence worth,' he reckoned.

Pleasure-garden entertainment was relatively old-fashioned, tailored for the more genteel clientele which made up the bulk of the first growth in tourism. By the 1890s things were on a different footing as the working class began to

Pierrots performing in the public park, Dunbar, *circa* 1920s.
Park concerts were a feature of the inter-war summer seasons and,
as in the case of Glasgow Parks venues, were not only at
the seaside. (Scottish Life Archive)

flock to resorts in their thousands. In Rothesay, for example, it was claimed that in August 1891 the resident population of 9000 was supplemented by as many as 30-40,000 visitors.

By the early 1900s substantial civic investments were being made in purpose-built seaside entertainment venues, replacing more ramshackle wooden pitches. The Dunoon Pavilion, for example, built in 1905, was a multi-purpose venue showing summer seasons of variety with

tearooms and a dance-floor for at least 800. In Portobello, Dundonian magician Harry Marvello in 1907 bought the Tower Hotel: 'I saw the possibilities of a piece of ground included with the hotel, so I floated a small company and built the Tower Pavilion there. We could seat 1000 and soon we were giving special nights to good houses.' Portobello became a centre for entertainment with the 27-acre Marine Gardens built in 1910, and Marvello recalled Peter Higgins'

pub on the promenade as a favourite port of call for music-hall folk: 'He had a big collection of photographs of star artistes round his walls and a fine visitors' book.'

The Pierrot craze which swept Britain in the 1890s had reached Aberdeen by the 1900s and troupes of Catlin's Royal Pierrots (part of a chain dominating the British summer scene) played Aberdeen in 1905 and 1906. In 1905 the council saw fit to build a modest wooden and corrugated iron Beach Pavilion and it was run by comedian David Thomson with three shows daily. It was here that another comedian, Harry Gordon, won a talent competition in 1908, going on to make regular professional appearances until in 1924 he took over the lease of the Beach Pavilion and produced his own summer seasons. These were so successful that in 1928 the town council replaced the wooden pavilion with a more permanent structure. Gordon's seasons continued until the war brought the business to an end in 1940.

Most of the seaside business was on the west coast, however, and in the 1920s and '30s was dominated by three families: the Fyfes, Kemps and Popplewells.

Brothers John and Robert Fyfe, partners in a Glasgow painting and decorating business specialising in theatre scenery painting, turned impresarios in 1903 with a company of entertainers in an open-air pitch on Rothesay esplanade. Business prospered and soon they were running a touring company around the Scottish resorts. By 1912 they were in a position to build their own cine-variety venues at Galashiels and Forfar. In the 1920s they leased theatrical property in Glasgow, bought the Star Palace Variety Theatre in Partick and refitted it as a dance hall, the F & F Palais, and in 1924 they took over the lease of the Rothesay Winter Gardens Pavilion. The latter was a venue built largely to their specifications and where, for over 20 summer seasons, they ran their popular and successful Rothesay Entertainers.

George Kemp was a travelling showman from Leicester who in 1899 saw the opportunities offered by moving pictures. Where 20 years earlier he might have moved into music hall, in 1913 he opened the La Scala Cinema in Saltcoats, going on to take over several other venues on the west coast. His son Harry, however, wanted to start a concert party. In 1922, in the face of opposition from his father who felt it was too risky, he took on a concert party for six weeks at La Scala. The show was a success and further concert party summer seasons followed in 1923 and 1924 when the 'Scotch Broth' revue went on tour, breaking box-office records across Scotland. The Kemps went on to expand both the cinema and concert party business, running shows in Largs, Saltcoats, Troon and Dunoon during the 1930s.

Like the Kemps, the Popplewells had come up from England. Ben Popplewell, a Bradford stockbroker, had in 1901 taken a sabbatical from the family business to join a pierrot troupe on the sands at Clacton-on-Sea, opening his own venue near Bradford in 1905. In 1913 he gave up stockbroking altogether and went up to manage the Pavilion Theatre Ayr, a municipally-owned theatre built in 1911, known locally as 'The White Elephant on the Green'. In 1925 he took over the Gaiety Theatre in Ayr, taking his two sons, Leslie and Eric, into partnership. At first business was slack and in 1927 they converted the Pavilion to a ballroom to avoid competition from a beefed-up programme at a revamped Gaiety. With their 1928 'Grand Vaudeville Season' they began a policy of engaging top performers, including Will Fyffe and Harry Lauder. By 1932, renamed 'The Gaiety Whirl', a long-running tradition of superior variety shows was established drawing both holidaymakers and locals.

The business was established enough for them to run parallel variety seasons in the Pavilion in the early 1930s, and business accounts for the two 1932 summer shows give a useful sense of the variations in the scale of seaside productions in general. Typically there was a small dancing troupe, a principal comedian with perhaps a feed and *soubrette* (which in this case meant female feed and all-rounder), a tenor and soprano, and possibly a musical act or sister act, as well as a pianist or even a small band – the size of cast depended on the nature of the venue. At the prestigious and more expensive Gaiety, the June 1932 cast numbered 35, including a named ten-piece band, separate producer and assistant producer, eight dancers and six 'chorus ladies'. The principal comedian, Dave Willis, was drawing £45 a week and the show cost a total of £317. 10s. At the Pavilion the total was £121. 10s. Principal comedian Charlie Kemble was on £25, having to double-up as producer and make do with a cast of eleven, a pianist-accompanist and no dancers.

Many seaside venues were even more modest. Bud Flanagan played a summer season in the early 1920s in East Wemyss on the Fife coast:

An Italian ice-cream merchant owned the pitch and had built a lovely stage on the beach with a soda parlour adjoining. We charged sixpence per deck chair and went on to 'bottle' – which means going around with collecting boxes among the people who stood on the edge of the pitch and didn't pay for chairs. We were a big success and became great favourites with the locals and holidaymakers .... At the end of the season, we had over £60 which we had snatched out of 'bottle'. It was nearly all in coppers with the odd silver threepenny bit.

REVELS" SALTCOATS 1932

GLASGOW
AND LARGS

HARRY KEMP'S SCOTCH BROTH ENTERTAIN

LA SCALA · SALTCOATS.

J. E. Sutton.   Ida McLeish   Robt. MacWray.   Willie Lindsay
Sylvia Watt.   Topsy.   Pete Davis   Trixie.

HARRY KEMP PRESENTS "SCOTCH BROTH" ENTERTAINERS

Further down the professional ladder many aspirants began their careers busking on the sand or, in the case of comedian George West at the start of his career, playing the flat roof of a beach-side gents.

For many resorts the arrival of the summer shows was a major event. In Leven, for example, which had substantial productions in both the Beach Pavilion and Jubilee Theatre, the *Leven Advertiser and Wemyss Gazette* reported the arrival of the 1936 season's entertainers in detail:

> *Mr. Gillespie [a local businessman turned impresario] arrived with his entertainers on Sunday evening direct from the New Metropole Theatre Glasgow. All the artistes are looking forward to their opening night on Friday, 3rd July. Some of the principals of the company went out golfing on Monday, and the newcomers to Leven spent their leisure time viewing Leven's landmarks, accompanied by a well-known citizen of the town. The company are delighted at the way the council have redecorated and refreshed the interior of the Beach Pavilion ….*

The Scottish summer seasons were long, up to 14 weeks, which gave a substantial boost to local economies. Not surprisingly, the departure of entertainers at the end of the season was another significant date in many a resort's calendar. The *Gourock Times* devoted a long article to the 1950 departure of comedian and impresario Alec Finlay's troupe, regulars at Cragburn Pavilion:

'FINLAY'S FROLICS'
SAY 'FAREWELL TO GOUROCK'

> *… Many of the artistes have made friends of local folk but these are nothing compared with the huge number to whom the Cragburn artistes are now firm favourites …. A charming little ceremony took place at the meeting of the local Old Age Pensioners Association when the old folks (they have been preparing for it for a long time) made a presentation to Mr & Mrs Alec Finlay.*

Though a season's contract guaranteed three months work, it was a demanding schedule with shows twice nightly, and a change of programme twice weekly making up to 28 separate programmes for which material had to be devised and rehearsed. The summer season in Scotland was regarded as a hard, but valuable training. Acts had to be versatile with up to 14 items per programme having to be spun from often small casts. As Renée Houston recalled of a 1916 Rothesay season at the start of her career:

> *You played everything from singing and dancing to dramatic sketches and knock-about comedy. It was*

Punch and Judy show, Rothesay, late 1940s. Punch and Judy shows are
part of a once diverse popular puppetry presence. There were
permanent puppet theatres (Mumford's in Glasgow was established in
the 1830s), and elaborate marionette companies, presenting anything from
pantomime to melodrama, toured the UK and appeared in
Scottish music halls into the early twentieth century. Punch and Judy,
once common on city streets, has largely retreated to the seaside.
(Scottish Life Archive)

a theatrical education which all the charm schools and drama schools in the world couldn't begin to equal. I played old ladies, young women, babies, the lot. I had a coloratura voice so I sang every kind of song. And I could also dance well …. I learned Scottish dancing from a dear little fellow who played the bagpipes and he taught me the fling, the reel, sword dancing and everything. And then I went on point and did ballet, while all the time I was learning my craft.

Programmes were the familiar revue mix of popular song and dance, together with Scotch song and dance and comedy sketches geared to the resort's clientele. Inevitably, given the need to keep 'changing', programmes were somewhat formulaic. Routines and sketches became well enough known that members of the cast were expected to run through them with little or no rehearsal. Renée Houston remembered some nights when the show was running early, having to go on to 'fill the time' since closing early risked a disgruntled audience who wanted value for money: 'Anyway, Charlie [Kemble] and I would go on. Invariably, we would play two old Glasgow women in a tenement building, arguing.'

Charlie Kemble, a Scottish seaside stalwart, was known for his ability to improvise, becoming renowned for his 'Fal al a diddle song', with its references to members of the audience apparently spun together 'on the spot', but most likely drawn from a carefully amassed stock. Years of working such shows gave a sixth sense about what would go down well with audiences. Correspondence between Greenock scriptwriter Bill McDonnell and Colin Murray, of double act Clark and Murray, goes into great detail about what exactly the duo wanted for their 1950 Rothesay season. Colin writes to Bill that he thinks the idea of a 'Rothesay song' is good and likes the idea of a reminiscence routine. He commissions Bill to work on the idea and describes how he envisages it working: Grace and he will come on singing the Rothesay song, then start talking about their first visit to Rothesay. He suggests various elements that could be brought into the patter: the old tram cars, the room and the kitchen with six beds (typical accommodation for working-class holidaymakers), and so on.

Shortly afterwards he writes in response to Bill's submission. His comments make clear just

how well audiences knew their acts, and the acts in turn knew their audiences. He rejects Bill's idea, giving the reason that whenever Grace appeared as a 'Wee girl' (one of their trademark routines), he must appear as her Daddy – and everywhere they went in Rothesay people shouted 'that's my Daddy' or 'I love my Daddy'. He reckoned that any break from the 'Daddy' character (like that in Bill's suggested routine) would be fatal.

In St Andrews, like Carnoustie, one of the posher golfing resorts, Falkirk producer Dave Hunter tailored his approach as follows:

> It had to be a very clean show because … the type of people that came to St. Andrews were a little bit that way …. Husbands golf daft, and the mothers and children came to the entertainers. So everything had to be spotless and clean. We wrote our own material and an awful lot of the material came from the people, wherever they came from ….
> I always got the name of the players, and I wrote little songs about the fathers, and always brought in what we term a closeness with the mothers and children ….

He was always on the lookout for some gimmick to promote and attract custom:

> … if business were a wee bit quiet you boosted it up with something. I had a boat down at St. Andrews

and I had a big name on, the summer concert party, you know, and lots of people went down to see the boat and have a look at it and say 'Oh, must go and see the show', you know. We'd comedy things on it, 'Please don't take this boat away'.

No amount of showmanship, however, could compete with the weather. As showbusiness journalist Rex King wrote of the 1947 season:

'KING SOL'S BIG BLOW FOR SCOTS COAST ENTERTAINERS'

… Glorious sunshine that has gladdened the hearts of holiday-makers has meant something approaching disaster to theatrical entertainers in Scotland's halls and beach pavilions. The summer of 1947 has been the most disastrous in living memory for many people in the show business. Promoters have dropped thousands of pounds. Shows have been taken off weeks ahead of schedule. Artistes have been asked to accept salary cuts.

As he goes on to suggest, however, it was not only the weather that was causing the down-turn. Post-war austerity was kicking in:

Today there is a thoughtful look in promoters' eyes as they lick their wounds. 'The boom is over' one of them told me: 'During the war, all sorts of people had money to burn, and business cashed in. Even a

year ago, things were still good, because thousands of demobbed men and girls were on holiday with gratuities burning a hole in their pockets. When the boom was on prices sky-rocketed. Small beach pavilions, which used to earn a summer rental of about £50 shot up to £250 for a season …. The artistes too cashed in …'.

He concludes ominously: 'Obviously there will have to be drastic cuts and changes in the whole set-up of summer show business …'. One of Bill McDonell's correspondents writing in March 1948 seems to confirm the sense of a chill:

This year Bowie has all the shows, except Dunoon Gardens, Carnoustie and nobody wants Millport. There will be no show at Cragburn and Wood even wanted to cut Jimmy Wallace's money for Perth – although he played to capacity. Galt does all the booking and they seem to be very much the one concern, as everybody is cut considerably – take it or starve.

The Fyfes had already pulled out of the seaside business in 1946, and by 1950 Leven was down to one small show. Within a few years post-war austerity was followed by a more decisive blow. Just as cheap train fares had brought audiences to the Scottish resorts, so, from the 1960s, cheap air fares took them away to the Costas.

'Aladdin' at the Royal Princess Theatre, Glasgow, 1881. This production
drew enthusiastic praise from the *Quiz*'s 'Cantankerous Critic':
'There is so much "go" in "Aladdin" that you can see it again and
again and enjoy it as often as you see it. There is but one hitch –
the incapacity of the house to contain its patrons.' (*Quiz*)

PANTOMIME

In the 1930s and '40s, a performer with contracts for the pantomime and summer season had two-thirds of their date book filled. Scottish pantomimes tended to be longer than in England, running for over 20 weeks. Given that they often re-used much of the same cast each year, there was the promise of more work the next winter. Dancer George Clarkson played eleven consecutive pantomimes at the Glasgow Queen's Theatre from early December to mid March and, in the case of the 1937/38 'Bluebeard', as late as 18 April, alternating this with long summer seasons in the Scottish resorts. In 1956, writer E G Ashton stated the reason for so much winter work:

> *Scotland is, quite simply, pantomime daft. There are vast lavish shows in the cities; the quick homely-humoured twice-nightlies; the busy touring shows; the home-made frolics ... and some hundreds of amateur productions ... in a 16 week run, one large Glasgow production alone will have played to close on a quarter of a million people. Audiences travel from fishing hamlets, mining villages, country towns, and even from one city to another in order to see a pantomime – and there have been 'three-in-a-day' bus trips, which take in the morning performance at the circus, a pantomime matinee, and another pantomime at night, without leaving any permanently damaging after-effects.*

Like many others, Ashton argued that pantomime was Scotland's real national drama. Yet until the middle of the nineteenth century there was little to distinguish it from British pantomime as a whole. The tradition had evolved from mid eighteenth-century dumb shows (hence mime), drawing on comic characters from the *Commedia dell'Arte*, notably Harlequin. These entertainments were shown all year round in smaller theatres without a licence for spoken drama. The first Harlequinade in Glasgow appears to have been in September 1751: 'A Pantomime Entertainment called "Harlequin Captive, or the Dutchman Bitt",' at Burrell's Close as part of a concert of vocal and instrumental music. By 1808 pantomime was well enough established for Walter Scott (who was involved in a scheme to put the Edinburgh Old Theatre Royal 'on a good footing') to complain to playwright Joanna Baillie, 'I cannot believe people would be brutes enough to prefer the garbage of melo-drama and pantomime to the high tragic feast ....'

As the earlier knockabout and acrobatic Harlequinade gradually lengthened, it became associated with the Christmas holiday season (with an almost continuous winter run between 1824 and 1859 at the Edinburgh Old Theatre Royal). The spotlight shifted from Harlequin to Clown, a move initiated by the celebrated Joey Grimaldi (who visited Edinburgh and Glasgow in the summer of 1816), and by the middle of the century pantomime had acquired its fairy-tale plots, casts of characters, and the familiar village and transformation scenes, with the Harlequinade as a subsidiary endpiece.

The first move to something more Scottish was the habit of sprinkling performances with local references. In 1810 we have in Perth 'The Magic Cave, or The Harlequin in Scotland'; and in 1811 the Edinburgh Theatre Royal staged a 'Harlequin in Leith'. By the 1850s there were complaints from critics about the adulterating effect of topical and local allusions, initiating a tradition of bemoaning the death of 'true' pantomime which has run ever since.

In the more upmarket theatres it was often a case of referring to local businessmen, with perhaps a little discreet advertising, and a good dose of middle-class civic pride. Her Majesty's Opera House in Aberdeen's 1872/3 'Little Goody Two Shoes' is credited as 'written by Wm. Bough Esq. The local points from Local Pens'. It makes reference to Pratt & Keiths, a large store, and has the following profession of love from 'Colin' to 'Goody':

> *My love for her will never be diminished;*
> *'Twill last until our New Post Office is finished,*
> *Last till Duke Gordon's statue grows both worn*
>   *and hoary;*
> *Last till a Bridge un-toll'd is built across the Torry.*

It is difficult to know how 'local' performances were. The scripts that survive give no idea of the unscripted elements which could so influence the character and atmosphere of a performance: ad-libbing, style of delivery (lines printed in English but spoken in Scots), whether players were local or not. Also, they tell us nothing of the many more humble shows, like Hughie Smith's 'fit-up' in Arbroath. As a local thespian recalled:

> *Hughie's pantomime created much stir in the Fore and Back Abbey Streets and in the purlieus of Barber's Croft. Joy upon joy rained upon the youngsters as they stepped gaily across the front platform to receive each an orange at ingoing. A clown with a red poker appeared in front to captivate the masses …. A famous fishcadger was taken in to play a part in the pantomime and made a droll and side-splitting 'bobby'. During the piece the urchins roared over this dainty couplet of the widow's:*

> > *Aha! my lad*
> > *Ye needna blaw;*
> > *I ken by yer feet*
> > *You're plain Jock Law.*

It does seem, however, that pantomimes took on a more thoroughly 'Scottish' flavour over the second half of the century. In Edinburgh the scripts by actor-playwright William Lowe drew on Scottish literature and folklore for stories, and in the venerable European dramatic tradition of using 'regional' characters as comedians, had his comic characters scripted in Scots. Over in

Glasgow, H C Beryl and T W Charles commissioned Fred Locke to write the local 'hits' for the 1880/1 Royal Princess pantomime on the south side of the city. Locke went on to write the thoroughly localised librettos for at least 16 further consecutive pantomimes, helping to establish a distinctively Scottish tradition at this theatre which lasted into World War II.

More than the script, however, the most important factor in making pantomime 'Scottish' was the involvement of music-hall performers. Prior to the emergence of the Scotch comics (discussed earlier) a comedy element was often provided by character actors from popular 'national drama'. As we have seen, the boundaries between theatre traditions were not fixed, and this was especially the case with pantomime (the 'Glen scene' which became a staple of Scottish pantomimes was, as Ashton put it, 'a fragment of our National Drama preserved in pantomime aspic'). Robert Pillans started in the 'free and easies', and played in both melodrama as well as pantomime in the 1860s and '70s. His 1872 song, 'Things are no' as they ocht tae be', ran to 20 verses of local gossip:

> *Since they've pooed a' the hooses doon,*
> > *oot by at Adam Square,*
> *I'm sure the Auld infirmary*
> > *will noo get lots o' air;*

W F Frame was one of the first popular comedians to appear in the more upmarket pantomimes, marking a move to seasonal respectability and enhanced earnings for subsequent generations of Scottish performers.

The new ane at the Meadow Walk
I doot we'll never see,
They tak' sae lang tae settle noo
hoo matters ocht tae be.

In the 1870s pantomimes in the number one venues across Britain began to import top music-hall stars in a more systematic fashion. A successful, long-running show could be highly lucrative, and impresarios would stake large investments hoping to attract the public with the lavishness of their productions. One of William McFarland's first ventures, on taking over his Dundee Alhambra venue in 1870, was to mount a Christmas show, billing it as 'McFarland's £600 Pantomime, Little Red Riding Hood'. But however much money was spent, getting the right combination of ingredients was tricky. Business was bad at the Glasgow Theatre Royal's 1881/2 'Dick Whittington', despite having popular 'national drama' actor Mr Gourley playing the role of Luckie 'with the pawky Scotch humour for which he is famous'. As the *Quiz's* so-called 'cantankerous critic' put it:

I have heartily enjoyed seeing the spirited manner
in which the actors and actresses have faced down
the effect of empty benches with redoubled smiles
and vivacity. Their term of endurance is now

drawing to a close, for Mr. Bernard announces the 'last nights' of his pantomime; and, better late than never, has, by reducing his prices … given himself a chance of coming in at the finish neck-and-neck with the other theatres.

Casting a top music-hall performer became almost a necessity for box-office success and the appearance of Scotch comics in the bigger theatres, usually in the dame role, reflected their growing power to draw. By the 1890s a long pantomime was part of the calendar for the top Scottish comedians, and has been ever since. W F Frame's 1890 debut as Maggie Muckle-moo at the Princess was a sign of the growing acceptance of these performers. As he recalled:

The author, Fred Locke was present and 'took my measure for the book,' which was well written. There is no doubt that it was one of the best and funniest of the many he wrote, and the pantomime was one of my greatest successes.

Frame played the following year at the Princess before moving on to the Theatre Royal in Edinburgh, with a show also written by Locke, where he played several more successful seasons. He was replaced at the Princess by J B Preston who, as Kirsty Cleishmaclaver in the 1894/5 'Babes in the Wood', sang 'I hivna come

Comedian Sammy Murray was known best for his dame roles in the Glasgow Queen's Theatre pantomimes. As one obituarist wrote on his death in 1949, 'Sammy Murray did not need to say anything funny. His appearance and facial expressions were sufficient to "crack" the coldest of audiences.' (School of Scottish Studies/Mabel Hall)

across yin yet', a typically full-blooded piece of Glaswegiana:

> *Noo, at the Tug of War oor Glesga' polis*
> *they got bate,*
> *Tho' they were na' very easy for tae lick;*
> *Altho' they canna' haul a rope they're raley*
> *up to date,*
> *At haulin' up a fellow tae the 'Nick'*
> *They'll staun up in a polis coort and open*
> *up their mooth*
> *An rap it in gey hard against some poor*
> *misguided youth*
> *I've heard o' several polismen that always*
> *tell the truth,*
> *But I've never come across yin yet.*

Mr Beryl's assistant, Rich Waldon, who took over the theatre in 1888, went on to write and produce the pantomimes featuring the next generation of Glasgow comedians. These included, from 1906, Peter Bermingham, remembered for his 'immaculate Glesca accent' and for yelling 'I've nae chinge, keep the hoarse' to his off-stage stooge. Waldon's assistant, Harry McKelvie, took over in 1919 and concentrated on the business side, introducing block bookings, sending invitations to works and offices, and providing tea and cakes for the big parties which were to become a regular fixture. Under his management the show ran from December until the theatre closed for the summer in May, opening for a short autumn Variety season before the next pantomime.

Unlike Waldon, who carefully scripted his shows, McKelvie left them to his performers. He kept an eye out for local talent, however, giving celebrated comedian Tommy Lorne an early boost to his career. He also spotted the comedian most associated with the theatre, George West, who played for 20 consecutive seasons, writing and producing many of the shows. These had the usual stock characters, but went in for original plots that showcased the principal comic with his distinctive gestures, mastery of facial expression and famously eccentric costumes. People did not go for a particular pantomime story, but to see George West year after year (there was even a fan club badge for him), and he arranged it so that he was on the stage most of the time. His daughter remembers the thrill of waiting in the dressing room far back down a corridor as he walked down to the stage:

> *You used to wait for it, and sometimes the orchestra*
> *would vamp, he'd maybe be coming on as Mae West*
> *and … this ROAR when he went on. And he*
> *would have to stand for ages waiting, the orchestra*
> *still vamping, before he could get started … they loved*
> *him, they absolutely loved him. And he never let*
> *them down.*

Glasgow Queen's Theatre pantomime cast. With virtually the same performers from
year to year, these faces became very well-known.

Often audiences would not let the show finish on time and brought sandwiches in their handbags, knowing that they would be having far too good a time to want to leave.

The Princess was only one of several long-running pantomimes with repeated appearances by particular Scotch comics and their loyal audiences. A striking example was the Queen's in the centre of Glasgow, perhaps the only other theatre to have quite as cultish a following as the Princess.

Though it struggled for the rest of the year, under proprietor Harry Hall this 'number three' theatre developed a style all of its own from the first pantomime in 1932 through to the late 1940s. It revolved around not only a familiar principal comic, local east-ender Sammy Murray in his Sarah Bell dame role, but almost an entire cast which reappeared year after year. Together with a rich garnish of local references, stylised Glasgow patois and risqué gags (occasionally attracting the attentions of the Lord Chamberlain's office to which all scripts had to be submitted), the Queen's panto developed a mythic status that reviewers of the show (with their 'proletarian pantomime' and 'real slice of Glesca') never failed to reflect and nourish. This reputation made up for the show being less lavishly staged than rival productions and guaranteed audiences including students and visitors from the West End who, attracted by the myth, came to 'slum it' in evening dress, much to the annoyance of the management. The 1937/8 'Bluebeard' broke the record for twice-nightly pantomimes with a 19-week run and over 187,000 customers paying for admission to 243 houses.

Among the show's most ardent admirers was theatre columnist Jack House, whose review of the 1940/1 'Humpty-Dumpty' gives a vivid description of a typical war-time effort:

If you haven't observed the funny side of an air-raid warning, I recommend a visit to the Queen's Theatre at Glasgow Cross, where the city's first panto has just opened. Scene is a kitchen, complete with recess-bed, occupied by Doris Droy and 'child'. Off go the sirens; out of bed leaps Doris; struggles into her stays and other garments, and then outside to the shelter. There's no room for faither (Billy Fields). Doris is unconcerned about him, except for the sudden thought: 'Whit wid we dae for the buroo money if ye wir killt?' Sam Murray (dame) remarks that when her hoose was bombed she and her old man were blown into a field – 'first time we've been oot thegither fur 30 years.' Other topical touches in this real Glesca show – top price is 3d, worth double the money – are an evacuee skit; a catty knitting bee; discourse between Doris and Sam as tram conductresses ….

The end of the Princess pantomime in 1944/5, Edinburgh Theatre Royal's in 1946 (in each case after six decades or more of pantomime), and then the closure of the Queen's Theatre in 1952, seemed to signal a watershed. They were followed by two difficult decades of closure and cut-back in the Scottish variety business as a whole. However, pantomime was always more flexible and had broader appeal than variety, particularly in the case of the more lavish spectaculars.

The outstanding purveyor of these shows was the Howard and Wyndham company. Mr and Mrs Wyndham had staged their first pantomime in Edinburgh in 1851, and son Fred had his first in 1888. They established a reputation for the scale and expense of their productions, bringing the cream of the music-hall profession to play in theatres and presenting them to audiences who might not otherwise set foot in a theatre, let alone a variety theatre. The company brought out a book in 1947, *Sixty years of Pantomime*, proudly recording all their Glasgow and Edinburgh productions. Vesta Tilley recalled students' night at the Theatre Royal, Glasgow:

The students booked the whole of the Gallery and gave an impromptu concert before the curtain rose on the pantomime. They fixed a steel wire from the Gallery to stage, and as the performers entered, down the wire came a more or less acceptable present for each principal, a bouquet for the ladies, a bottle of whisky for the comedians, and a dead cat for the Demon King.

Artistes and audience thoroughly entered into the spirit of the 'rag', and although the performance was unduly prolonged, all went smoothly. It rather alarmed me when, on reaching the stage door, I found that the students had unharnessed the horses from my conveyance and insisted on dragging me back in the carriage to my hotel.

Harry Lauder, building on his first major successes in London, 'arrived' as a popular favourite in Britain with his 1905 appearance in 'Aladdin' at the Glasgow Theatre Royal in 1905. There he broke in his song 'I love a lassie' with such success that it held up the action while the audience joined in:

*I think it ran for thirteen weeks, and we played to packed houses. All Glasgow went mad about this pantomime; even the railway companies ran special trains from the districts so that the people could see Harry Lauder as 'Roderick McSwankey' ....
Howard and Wyndham had got together a perfect combination of artistes for its presentation ....*

The Glasgow Alhambra developed a similar reputation for the scale of its productions. The Alhambra started pantomimes in 1917, and initially had no Scottish headliners, but soon succumbed to the necessity for a top Scotch comic dame (despite having switched from variety to musicals in 1926). Under the management of Tom Arnold there was a 16-season run by Harry Gordon from 1937, in partnership with Will Fyffe and then Alec Finlay. The tradition continued after the war featuring the next generation of comics like Jimmy Logan, Stanley Baxter and Rikki Fulton.

The mix of extravagant production and top Scotch comic was a crowd-puller. One reviewer of the 1949/50 'Dick Whittington' (according to Tom Arnold, 'the most lavish pantomime ever produced in Scotland') commended producer Robert Nesbitt for managing to combine 'London's own fairytale with Scotland's own brand of comedians. He has even added Italian musical clowns and acrobats', concluding 'only pantomime could assimilate this mixture …'. But for another reviewer, the mix did not work so well:

Harry Gordon as the Dame seems to have discarded a little of that talent he has to be funny in order to appear more as a clothes-horse than a comedian. His costumes, of which there are many,

are all magnificent, beautifully cut, and exquisitely designed …. Their very elegance is a brake upon the exuberance of the Laird of Inversneckie, whom we would rather see as comic than as mannequin.

This challenge has always faced pantomime: to be glitzy and yet homely – one given greater intensity with the rise of television. Being a mongrel genre, pantomime has proven resilient, undergoing continuous tinkering and more wholesale adaptation up to the present. Notable examples include the 1950 'The Tintock Cup' at the Citizens Theatre (housed in the former Princess) which, coming from a 'legit' background, mixed literary Scottish story with traditional pantomime business and Scots-comic-dame sketches; and Howard and Wyndham's 'Jamie' pantomimes of the early 1960s which attempted to get away from the already tired borrowing of television and radio personalities, and return to revitalised roots with a Scottish story and kaleidoscope of tartanry.

Its adaptability has enabled pantomime to survive in Scotland in several guises. While the number of smaller scale variety-style shows has declined, pantomime has become a refuge for the Scottish variety tradition in productions in the few remaining variety theatres and newer civic venues built since the war. Large-scale performances have continued, still headlining Scottish comedy from various backgrounds alongside the ubiquitous sports and soap opera stars.

Amateur dramatic societies' annual pantomimes are in some ways heir to the couthier shows of the variety era with their high proportion of local talent. There are dozens of amateur productions each year, often the only accessible pantomime for many rural areas. Generally they have traditional plots geared towards the children who make up much of the audiences and casts. Given the closeness of audience and players, there is a very different atmosphere from the large professional shows, with far more local jokes and mentions of people in the audiences rather than in the news or on television.

For many smaller, unsubsidised amateur companies, the annual pantomime provides brisk business. Edinburgh Peoples' Theatre (founded in 1943) has produced pantomimes for over 40 years, running for two weeks or so in December. Together with their Edinburgh Festival show this helps fund the rest of the year's activities. By contrast, Falkirk Children's Theatre is a large joint civic-voluntary venture. It has produced 28 annual shows with casts of up to 120, playing for ten performances in the town hall with 1000 people per house and, for the last year, televised in edited form. The 'book' is full of the usual local allusions, a recent example sending up the flurry of UFO interest around Bonnybridge and set in space, called 'Snow White and the Seven Wee ETs'.

The Falkirk Children's Theatre production of 'Snow White and the Seven Wee ETs' in December 1997. (Terence Hughes Photography)

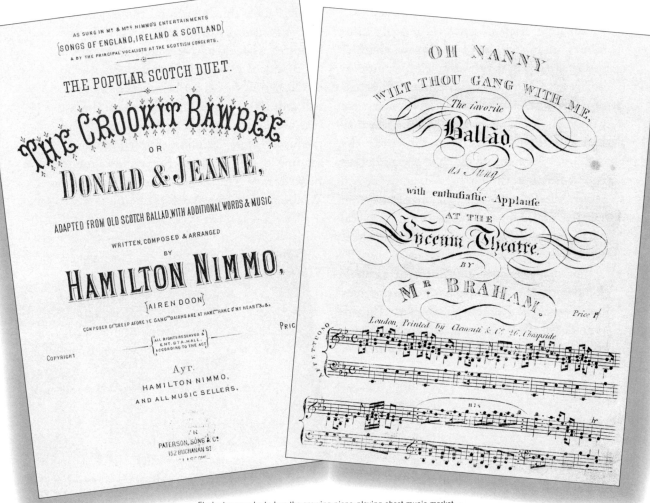

Flashy typography to lure the growing piano-playing sheet music market —
John Braham was one of the most celebrated British tenors of
the early nineteenth century, and Hamilton Nimmo and wife were one of the many
acts to tour with Scottish 'song entertainments' from the middle of the century.

SCOTTISH SONG AND MUSICAL ACTS

Scottish popular song, like English and Irish, had long circulated around the whole of Britain: eighteenth-century London chapbooks and broadsides included Scottish and Irish songs, and their Scottish and Irish counterparts included English hits. By the middle of the nineteenth century, improved transport and steam printing meant that singers and song sheets travelled rapidly (one of the earlier examples of technical innovation impacting on popular culture). In the proto-music halls with their high proportion of vocalists, just as in the earlier convivial glee societies, singers of all types tried out the latest fashionable hits. John Wilson McLaren remembered the shopkeepers, clerks and soldiers who frequented Bryce's in Edinburgh favouring comic songs 'that had just become popular in the London music-halls', as well as sentimental and patriotic ditties, alongside comic Scots songs.

The history of much of what was sung in Scottish halls belongs to the history of music hall in general. Of more particular interest, however, are the trained professional specialists in Scottish song who became a fixture of music-hall bills and flourished into the television age.

The origins of this type of singer can be traced to the rise in the early nineteenth century of the 'respectable' concert entertainer. These trained soloists drew their repertoire from the melange of song generally known as parlour or drawing-room ballads, much of which were the permutations of 'folksongs' with written scores known as 'popular song' or 'national airs'. Scottish 'folksongs' had been collected, refined and imitated since the beginning of the eighteenth century, gaining popularity throughout Britain as the century progressed, with growing numbers of bulky song collections published in both London and Scotland. Writing in 1761,

English antiquarian Bishop Percy claimed 'our most polite ladies … warble Scottish Airs'. This interest climaxed towards the end of the century with the publication of Johnson and Burns' 600-song *Scots Musical Museum*, followed by many more tomes of increasingly synthetic lyrics riding on the wave of enthusiasm generated by Walter Scott's popular antiquarianism.

This type of (not only Scottish) 'national air' became part of both the polite amateur and the professional repertoire in the drawing room, on the concert platform, in pleasure-garden recital rooms, and given the miscellaneous fare found in early nineteenth-century theatres, on the stage (often in Walter Scott adaptations). As we have seen, the boundary between high and low theatre was blurred. Penny booths had their Shakespeare reductions, and licensed theatres borrowed 'popular' elements of song, music and dance for dramatic presentations.

Covent Garden favourites like John Braham, Madame Vestris and Miss Stephens toured widely with numerous Scottish songs in their stock of favourites. In a July 1828 Glasgow Theatre Royal programme that included performances of Mozart's 'Marriage of Figaro' and the 'National Melo-drama "Rob Roy",' Miss Stephens gave renditions of 'There's a Bonny Briar Bush', 'Coming thro' the Rye' and 'Auld

Robin Gray' (a Scottish music hall amateur night staple).

This style of song and performance was further popularised by the mid-century boom in illustrated sheet-music publication for the amateur market of middle-class piano players, with songs puffed by association with stars: 'Donald MacLeod, An admired simple Scotch Ballad sung with the utmost applause by Mrs. Dickons at the Theatre Royal Lyceum ….'

Local talent was not slow to cash in on the Scots song fad. Having spent four years studying to be a precentor, John Templeton took the plunge into a theatrical career in England in the 1820s, building his reputation until he progressed to Covent Garden. In 1843 he turned to producing his own recitals, touring across Britain, Ireland and America with his 'Nicht wi' Burns' and 'The Rose, the Shamrock, and the Thistle'. When he died in 1886, he left a fortune of over £80,000. John Wilson, originally a compositor in Perth, secured a position as a precentor (choral leader) in Edinburgh, having studied under Italian teachers in London, and took to the stage in 1830 as Harry Bertram in an Edinburgh Old Theatre Royal production of 'Guy Mannering'. Covent Garden beckoned and thereafter highly lucrative tours in North America, including an 1849 visit to Canada with his 'Jacobite Entertainments', cut short by his death in the cholera epidemic of that year.

In the second half of the century the concert promotion business was developing rapidly across Britain. Daytime concerts, like the 1858 'Grand Morning Concert' in Bridge of Allan, were aimed at the cultural aspirations of the middle classes, particularly 'ballad concerts' with items from opera and oratorios as well as drawing-room ballads. This was far from the smoke-filled, male-dominated, urban, working-class music hall. But the two were opposite poles on an entertainment spectrum with much activity lying somewhere in between.

As we have seen, venues might host all types of performance. Clark's Dunfermline Music Hall opened in 1852 with a concert-style bill, with singers including a Miss Rainforth who, as the press notice put it, 'warbled out "Auld Robin Gray" in a most feeling and effective manner', and the band of the 42nd Highlanders. Soon after the opening John Templeton was booked, having recently appeared in the town with a lecture on the 'vocal art' and recital of 'favourite Scotch, English, and Irish songs, interspersed with self-told anecdotes and recitations by way of introduction'. The hall, Clark's *Journal* informs us, 'will afford him an opportunity of displaying his musical powers to better advantage'.

The shows presented by touring companies plying more conservative rural audiences were

a kind of hybrid, encapsulated in James Lumsden billing his 1878 visit to the Temperance Hall in Kirkwall as a 'National Ballad and Comic Entertainment'. Music-hall comedians had concert-platform singers of Scots songs in their concert parties and singer-impresarios borrowed suitable music-hall comedians. David Kennedy (another precentor turned concert platform success) employed the young music-hall comedian Harry Lauder in one of his many Kennedy family concert tours of Scotland.

This expanded concert activity in the second half of the century ran in tandem with, and drew much of its talents from, a burgeoning of organised amateur singing with the formation of numerous choral associations, the introduction of the more accessible 'tonic-sol-fa' system of notation (using the words 'doh ray me fa', *etc* instead of symbols), and prize competitions for songs and singers. Thomas Whammond's fictional letter to his parents from one such 'tonic-sol-fa' graduate about a prize competition in the 1880s, though comically exaggerated, seems nonetheless to be the fruit of actual observation:

… I was ushered into the presence o' as strange an' motley a groop as e'er my een beheld …. Ae frichtsome lukin' fallow, wha was tae represent a wild Eerishman, was cuttin' awfu' anticks on the

flure, whurlin' a shillelah abune his head, an' bawlin at the tap o' his voice, 'The March o' the callogen Men.' Frae the comicals I turned tae tak' a peep at the sentimentals. They were a' weel dressed, gentish-lukin' chaps, ilk ane airmed cap-a-pee wi' pitch-forks an' tremendous rolls o' musick paper. Every ane seemed determined on takin' the furst prize. Sic a hummin', hawin', clearin' o' throats, soondin' o' pitch-forks, rattlin o' musick paper, an' crunshin' o' 'Fiddledrum's Best Cough Lozenges', ye never heard a' yer days .... The singin' was commenced by a Mr McGraw, wha gied 'Bothwell Castle' wi' sic a vengeance, that had he been inside o' that auld an' venerable edifeece, I'm certain he wad hae brocht doon its 'ruined towers' aboot his lugs ....

This choral activity was partly the product of anxious middle-class sponsored 'rational recreation' aimed at moulding the leisure activities of the dangerous working classes and thereby introducing them to bourgeois values. 'Good Music' was seen as a valuable tool in this crusade, and in his *Scottish song: 'Its Wealth, Wisdom and Social significance'* (1889), Professor J S Blackie, an ardent promoter of the 'choicest' Scottish song, expounds at length on its socially 'harmonising' potential. These songs should not be left to the 'exercitation of a wandering ballad-singer, or the exhilaration of village types', but

'Aunt Kate's' Scottish Songbook, *circa* 1900. Popular magazine *The People's Friend* sold a variety of 'Aunt Kate' songbooks, and regularly included new Scottish songs in its columns.

taken up by 'a healthy national system of youthful training'. David Kennedy is singled out for particular commendation:

In Kennedy's musical evenings, given frequently in the Music Hall [ie the 'polite' concert chamber in the Assembly Rooms], Edinburgh, the hearty humour of the father and the graceful sweetness of the daughters, united to produce an aesthetical and a moral effect of the rarest kind ....

The middle decades of the century saw a craze for singing and writing Scots song that crossed class boundaries. Rev. Charles Roger's *The Scottish Minstrel: The songs and song writers of Scotland subsequent to Burns* (1870) gives potted biographies of writers across the social spectrum, from Lady Nairn, queen of the genre, to numerous ministers and lawyers, to shepherds, postmasters, rope-makers and vagrants. Despite the wide social spread of song-writers, these songs were remarkably homogenous: sentimental, nostalgic and pastoral. On the face of it, 'Scots song' was spectacularly successful in spreading middle-class aesthetics and the associated values.

'Rational recreation', however, ignores the extent to which people simply wanted to sing and make music for pleasure: there was no innate working-class disposition to be 'irrational', or to be writing any particular type of song. We cannot infer the triumph of bourgeois morality from the popularity of these songs since they probably meant different things to different audiences, singers or writers. A song decorously delivered in a west-end drawing room was not the same when sung as a communal anthem in the music hall. Music-hall and concert-party audiences had a taste for powerfully sentimental delivery, long after it lost favour in the concert hall. According to his obituary, tenor J M Hamilton's long popularity in the west of Scotland was due to the 'expression and fervour' with which he sang his speciality, the 'Auld Scots Sangs'.

Songwriters who appeared in edited collections with a 'healthy' sentimental or patriotic song might turn their hand to more overtly music-hall fare. John Pettigrew (1840-91), well-known in Glasgow as 'The Parkhead Minstrel', a gardener by trade until bronchitis brought him to the poorhouse, had lyrics published in the likes of Kyle's *Lyric Gems* and Roger's *Modern Scottish Poets*, as well as Daniel Barr's music-hall journal the *Professional*.

Singers of Scots songs were a hybrid group singing a mixed repertoire in a diverse range of settings. Late Victorians' lists of favourite singers encompassed opera stars like James Hislop and Durward Lely, graduates from busking such as

Helen Kirk, Gaelic song specialist and reputedly the first Highland woman to be recorded, Jessie MacLachlan, as well as local amateurs and the more vocally gifted Scotch comics. The traffic between the music hall and concert platforms defies categorisation. Glasgow concert promoter Walter Freer organised popular Saturday afternoon concerts for the Glasgow corporation's newly-acquired St Andrew's Hall in the 1890s, with regular appearances by top Scottish singers, instrumentalists and music-hall comedians, representing the high point of harmonisation between the music hall and concert platforms.

Of his youth in the 1850s, however, Freer tells us that with concerts priced out of reach for most people, his passion for singing, dancing, and instrument-playing drew him rather guiltily to the music halls:

It seems queer to me now that, concurrently with attending the Band of Hope, clan soirees, and the Glasgow Abstainers' concerts, I should have been putting in appearances at such houses as Shearer's, Whitebate's and Brown's …. Comparing these extraordinarily crude and rowdy entertainment parlours with our palatial modern theatres, I am amazed that they ever won any patronage whatsoever. But they were popular, and I used to sneak in often enough, and enjoy the warmth and fun … without any qualms of conscience.

Freer's 'qualms' probably stem from the fact that despite its success in presenting an elevated face, music-hall entertainment for many people remained the antithesis of Scots songs. Journalist Robert Ford (a prolific editor of Scottish song collections) fretted about country youth 'catching up the howling rhapsodies of the music halls only a day later than the people of the city'. In the foreword to her penny song-book, the *People's Friend*'s Aunt Kate worried that 'in these days of popular airs and music hall ditties there is just the possibility of our losing sight of our grand old Scottish songs' and speculated on the contempt Robert Burns would have had for 'the man who prefers the tawdry glitter of the catch-penny rhyme to the lasting brilliance of the gems of our national minstrelsy'.

Though the Scots song craze and wider 'ballad boom' had peaked by the turn of the century, the arrival of the gramophone and then radio maintained substantial audiences. Trained singers of Scots songs remained a staple of variety and concert party bills. Being more subject to fashion, the careers of comedians might wane, but tenor J M Hamilton, who made his debut on the Glasgow concert platform around 1877, was still active in the 1930s making frequent broadcasts.

The careers of more recent singers illustrate the continuing popularity of the various Scots

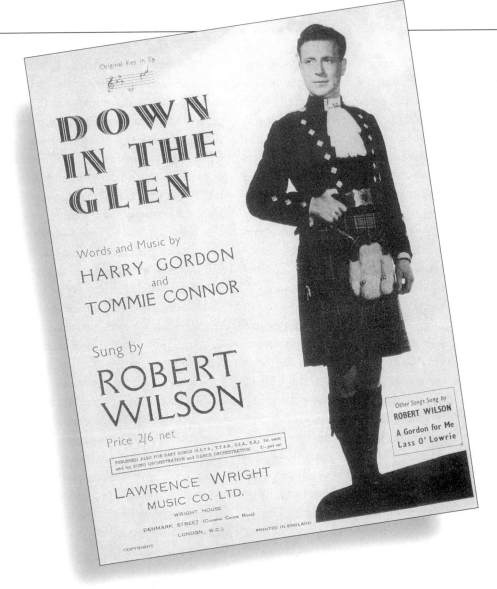

Sheet music for 'Down in the Glen', a song particularly associated
with 'The Voice of Scotland', Robert Wilson.

song specialists into the television age. Like so many of his Victorian predecessors, Cambuslang tailor's son Robert Wilson started out in local music competitions. He then studied with Glasgow Cathedral choirmaster Eliot Dobie and went on to work both on the recital platform with a spell in the D'Oyly Carte opera company and, from his debut with the Rothesay Entertainers in 1930, as an immensely popular variety artist, making numerous recordings, radio and latterly television appearances. Kenneth McKellar studied at the Royal College of Music in London, toured with the Carl Rosa Opera Company, and then concentrated on a career in Scots song, making numerous recordings and appearances in variety theatres, touring shows, and television. Moira Anderson, like Kenneth McKellar a music college graduate and host of her own television song shows, has made many recordings and appeared in summer seasons and pantomime. Andy Stewart, who reached a mass audience as host of 'The White Heather Club', specialised in a repertoire which overlapped with that of the Scots comic. As he puts it in his foreword to *The Andy Stewart Song-book:* 'The plaintive song that tugs at the heart and mists the eye; the sentimental ballad that sends us strolling down memory lane to years gone by; the comic number that brings a smile to every face ....'

These singers were in a long and vibrant tradition predating music hall, but have tended to suffer critical neglect as the gap between the worlds of classical and operatic song and the more popular repertoire has widened, while at the same time not being theatrical enough to engage the interest of theatre historians. They were also somewhat anomalous for post-war folk revivalists searching out the 'pure' tradition and its bearers. Ironically, many 'tradition' bearers often had a good smattering of Harry Lauder and parlour ballads in their repertoires and it was not long before variety theatres and touring shows were showcasing the new 'folk' acts like the 'Joe Gordon Folk Four' alongside the more familiar type of Scots singers.

As in the case of song, musical acts of all types were a feature of the popular theatrical stage with a particular emphasis on the novel or exotic. Since the eighteenth century, Scottish instrumental music had gone through a process of adaptation and 'refinement' for the stage and concert hall. By the second half of the nineteenth century a type of concert platform Scots fiddle virtuoso evolved, the pre-eminent example being Banchory-born James Scott Skinner. He was often elaborately kilted and played a style of Scots fiddle music adapted for the acoustics of large halls, to be listened to rather than danced to, with elements of non-traditional technique and flashy embellishment.

A graduate of touring company Dr Marks' Little Men, Skinner brought music-hall showmanship to Scots fiddle music learnt from traditional players, and for decades took concert parties around Scotland and abroad leaving a deep imprint through his recordings and books. For his Logie collection he received a glowing introduction from Professor Blackie, praising his 'noble work of giving to the world the Logie Collection of Scottish songs, pipe tunes, Strathspeys, &c. You could not spend your genius on a task at once more patriotic and more opportune', before going on to treat Skinner to a lecture on the 'great moral and educative value' of popular song (instrumental music, not having words, was not able to be quite so moral and educative).

Skinner's best-known successor, MacKenzie Murdoch, rose from the ranks of the Good Templars Harmonic Association and made his debut at one of Walter Freer's Corporation afternoon recitals. He then went on to tour with Willie Frame and Harry Lauder and made a number of gramophone recordings. Billed as 'The Scottish Paganini', he continued a tradition of showy instrumental playing which was already being abandoned from higher status concerts, but which, like 'the auld Scotch songs', remained popular on the music-hall stage not only with the violinists, but with concertina and accordion players.

MacKenzie Murdoch

The concertina had been a popular instrument with a range of music-hall acts, including a virtuosic style of performer initially popular on both concert platform and in the halls. In September 1888, virtuoso and inventor of his own fingering system, Professor MacCann, had twelve nights engagement at the Gaiety and Star in Glasgow, 'where he was received nightly with deafening applause', afterwards being engaged at the Glasgow Exhibition 'where the people flocked in thousands to see and hear him play'. His successor, Alexander Prince, was born into a Scottish professional musical family and established a career playing the whole range of late-Victorian popular taste, including elaborately arranged versions of Scottish song and dance tunes. Into the twentieth century, players like Walter Dale and his son Tommy both taught and played in dance bands and on the variety stage, including skilful adaptations of Scottish dance and, in particular, Scott Skinner compositions in their repertoires.

With the cinema and dancing crazes of the inter-war years, musical tastes diversified. Variety theatres reflected this, with top radio and recording acts and bands appearing at the 'number one' theatres. In smaller revues and seaside shows, local turns tried their hand as cowboy duos, Hawaiian serenaders, or whatever else was in fashion. In the 1926 revue 'First Edition' at the Alhambra, Leith, the musical items included two spots with Cissie Lang and her ukelele, violinist James Frame in 'Killarney Sunshine' and in the next spot as a 'Fiddlin' Cowboy', while Tommy Dale appeared as Gustavo the minstrel in a cabaret scene, in his own spot playing 'Faust in Foxtrot, Piccolo Solo on Concertina, A Little Surprise, Medley of Popular Airs', and later on in a tin-pan-alley selection.

Shows drew much musical talent from the amateur instrumental music scene which had been expanding since the middle of the nineteenth century. Late-Victorian Post Office directories show year by year proliferation of music teachers and shops selling mass-produced instruments and cheap collections of popular instrumental music. This growth continued up to World War II stimulated by radio, 78 rpm records and musical consumer products – accordions, banjos, mandolins, mouth organs – all serviced by magazines like *Popular Music and Dancing Weekly*, *Popular Music and Film Song Weekly* and *B. M. G.* ('Banjo, Mandolin, Guitar'). As the Depression took hold in the 1930s this hobby often became a source of income for back-court buskers and, for the more talented, on stage. One Glasgow amateur violinist, finding himself out of work in the 1930s, joined up with an accordionist and busked his way around

Ireland, returning to set up a band and perform in music halls and at local dances.

In the case of those playing Scottish music, fiddle and concertina were nudged aside by the accordion. This instrument, more than any other, has become identified not only with Scottish country dance, but with the Scottish variety business, and in particular the kilted 'teuchter' shows of the television era. This was found both in a continuing tradition of virtuoso performers like Will Starr, who played flawlessly executed strict tempo dances as well as elaborate continental-style showpieces, and in the various combinations of single, double, and singing acts like accordion and piano duo the Alexander brothers, a type of act well-suited to the Scottish touring cabaret and television shows that superseded the variety theatre business.

Accordion virtuoso Will Starr — Scottish amateur accordion champion aged ten, he went on to great renown in concerts, variety and television at home and abroad.

Ken Swan started ventriloquism as a hobby, appearing in Scout Gang shows.
He went into variety following a spell in ENSA during World War II,
toured at home and abroad in summer seasons and pantomime,
and latterly worked the clubs. Magee, the doll, acted the part of
a scruffy, worldly-wise naughty boy.

DANCE AND SPECIALITY ACTS

Though the history of music hall is dominated by comedians and singers, much of what was actually seen in theatres was drawn from the great diversity of other artistes, including dancers and those collectively known as speciality acts: magicians, acrobats, contortionists, jugglers, tightrope walkers, strongmen, and the more idiosyncratic trick cyclists, lightning cartoonists, and the like. A review of a night at the Glasgow Gaiety in March 1886 shows the range of a typical bill with its mix of exotically-named and often foreign speciality acts, with home-grown comedians and singers:

Mdlle. Rosa, the only lady ventriloquist on the boards, fairly brought down the house with her exceedingly well-worked entertainment .... Mr. George Beauchamp, character comedian, who has lately come back from America, scored a terrific success with several impersonations that he put on.

Miss Flo Chester, is a talented serio-comic vocalist. A genuine old favourite Glasgow comic, Mr. James Dunlop, has been doing well since he opened on Monday last. The Tyrolese trio, the Sisters Cassetti, are received with the greatest approbation at every appearance. Miss Georgina Forrester, Scottish ballad vocalist, has increased in favour since her first week .... Mr. Frank Hayward, descriptive and comic vocalist, continues to give the greatest satisfaction. Stebb & Trepp, continental grotesques, keep the audience in screams .... The Snowflake Ballet arranged by Tessy Guinness, has been nightly getting more popular ....

As discussed in the chapter on page 1, dance, acrobatics and other novelties and spectaculars were (like song and music) heavily 'puffed' in early nineteenth century theatrical programmes attempting to compete with a growing number of rival attractions, especially circus. A sequence of programmes presented in Kirkwall in the summer of 1830 has melodrama, Shakespeare and comic farces with songs and 'broad sword combats &c' interspersed with ballet dance interludes, including one called 'Tars on Shore; Or, the Kirkwall Landlady'. After the 1843 Theatre Act, however, these elements were increasingly banished from the 'legit' stage as it strived for greater 'artistic' status.

The singing saloons and 'free and easies' presented mainly vocal acts, but as they evolved and grew, music halls proved a natural home for more visual and physical acts. Touring troupes of usually Continental ballet and other dancers became common and, as in the case of the Sisters Ridgeway's visit to Whitebait's in 1875, were of great concern to those in a moral panic. Theatre managers were well aware of the erotic appeal of dancers, but presented them as adding an element of refinement to the bills (just as body-stockinged *tableaux vivants* were presented as 'artistic') and ballet dancing acts appeared regularly in theatres until the demise of variety.

Home-grown troupes of chorus dancers began to be established around the turn of the century to supply the packaged shows of the variety era. In their heyday from the 1920s to early '50s, most Scottish shows had between eight and 16 dancers. They were often supplied by dancing school proprietors like well-known

Edinburgh teacher Adelaine Calder known as Madame Ada, or assembled by particular producers like the 'Hamish Turner dancers', or performers like Tommy Morgan with his 'Morganettes' and the 'Lex McLean girls' run by his wife, dancer Grace Dryburgh.

Probably best known were those supplied by May Moxon. Coming from a theatrical family, she began her dancing career at the age of ten in 1917 at the Glasgow Casino cine-variety theatre in Argyle Street, also appearing in Henglers Circus in its annual Glasgow Christmas show. When a serious car accident ended her dancing career in the 1930s, she formed the first of her troupes of dancers, going on to supply theatres controlled by Galt's agency across Scotland and to expand her business. It is claimed that she employed as many as 1825 girls.

These troupes of dancers were highly trained to meet the varied demands and rapid programme changes of production variety in Scotland. As Moxon dancer May Morrison recalled:

In Scotland you had to be what you called an 'all-rounder'. You didn't get away with being an acrobat, or a ballet dancer or a tap-dancer. You had to have a bit of everything. When you went to dancing classes when I was a wee girl you were taught Highland, you were taught Irish dancing and you were taught ordinary tap. So you had to be an all-rounder.

This meant dancers could have enough pre-rehearsed material for their own spots and adapt to the multiple 'scena' format, usually co-ordinated by whatever individual dancing act was on hand with a minimum of rehearsal. By the 1950s, with theatres largely given over to long-running resident shows, the role of choreographer took on more importance. However, according to dancer turned producer/choreographer Billy Cameron, a lot depended on the head girl of a troupe and there was a good deal of *ad-hocism* and 'picking things up'. In the case of the ersatz 'Scottish dancing' it was 'more skipping around. Skip, change, step was done a lot and often Highland dancing came into it – pseudo Highland'.

As with every other aspect of the business there was something of a pecking order between these troupes. For example, the Glasgow-based Royal Caledonians, run by 'Gaggy' Campbell and continued by her daughter Agnes, were considered slightly classier, playing for Collins rather than Galts and appearing at number two venues like the Theatre Royal Edinburgh and Aberdeen Tivoli.

Of the numerous dance turns (hornpiping, clog-dancing, Highland sword-dancing and more eccentric permutations), many Scottish acts came from the well-established competition circuit. Edinburgh dance teacher and dancing-

The Jackson Sisters – Betty Jackson and Mabel Hall (*left*) started as a song and dance act in the early 1930s, specialising in show songs with elaborate costumes. Mabel got into the business at the age of 14 after a chance audition: 'I never seemed to have gone to get a lesson. I just travelled from then until I was fifty, and I've played all the theatres … I loved every minute of it.' (School of Scottish Studies/Mabel Hall)

troupe supplier Betty Brandon had been on the Highland dance circuit since the age of five, weekend after weekend, and specialised in training prize-winning dancers for the circuit, many of whom made variety theatre appearances. George Clarkson, the youngest of 18 children, was sent for dancing classes in Glasgow:

How my father and mother found the money to pay for my train fare into Glasgow to get these lessons I'll just never know .... I became a dancer and started first off round the Highland games, Cowal games, Braemar and the lot. I won quite a number of medals for my dancing, but my favourite dance was the sailor's hornpipe. I picked up many, many a gold medal for the sailor's hornpipe but the unfortunate part about it was that every medal that I won and every cup I won I could only see it from the Saturday to the Monday because it went a missing on the Monday and I discovered later on that they were in the pawn ....

Clog-dancing in particular seems to have inspired strong partisanship. An April 1899 clog-dancing contest, presided over by three local comedians at the Britannia in Glasgow, turned into 'a lively night' when it was announced that Michael Hannaway of Coatbridge had beaten Glasgow's J Harvey Daley: 'There was a terrific storm of yelling, hissing, howling .... Someone shouted out, "You're Irish". Hannaway retorted very sharply, "I can't help being Irish".' The judges had to retire and the uproar spilled out onto the street.

Moving into the twentieth century, although prize-winning Highland dancers (who ultimately came into their own in Scottish light entertainment television shows) might still appear on bills, it was American dance crazes that were most eagerly copied on the variety stage. This meant good business for the many dancing schools that opened. Glasgow in particular produced many Hollywood-inspired dance acts like the Americanised singing and dancing 'Sister acts' that were almost obligatory in variety bills across Britain in the 1930s and '40s: the Ardene Sisters, the Morrell Sisters, and Jackson Sisters all going on to tour the prestigious Moss Empires.

Most Scottish dance acts favoured the same dance styles as their English counterparts, especially tap-dancing. As Billy Cameron describes his act with Irene Campbell (daughter of Agnes), 'the main feature was pseudo-Fred Astaire and Ginger Rogers'. For most Scottish dancers, a 'Scottish act' was only a small part of their repertoire, possibly used for one week of a summer show and on the last night. For dancers who toured (and being what was called a 'dumb'

act they had good opportunities for this), a Scottish element was more important. Gail Leslie and George Clarkson (junior) were always asked to perform a kilted act abroad, and they developed a turn which began with a medley of 48 different Scots songs and went into dance, with Gail doing some tap in her kilt and then George doing some Highland dance.

Turning to the more exotic 'speciality acts' we find listed in the pages of *Who's who in Variety* (a good cross-section of the business compiled in 1950 by the official magazine of the Variety Artists' Federation, the *Professional*) the following Scots-born artists: *Adagio* dancers (a combination of slow dance, acrobatics, balancing and lifting) Babette and Raoul (Babette made her debut aged seven at the Glasgow Metropole); Lawrie Carton, lightning cartoonist; Billy Crotchett, comedy musician; Jack Francois, comedian and acrobatic dancer; Carmen Garcia of the three Graceful Garcias (acrobatic poseurs and dancers); Jack Melville, comedy juggler; The Mysterious Mysticus (quick-change artist Alan McKelvin from Inverness); bird mimic and whistler George McTear; James Watson of comic knockabout act Pop, White and Stagger; and Donald Younger of Younger and Younger, comedy acrobats.

These more physical performers were the most direct heirs of the itinerant tradition of usually Continental jugglers, tumblers and particularly rope-dancers, who had been appearing in Scotland for hundreds of years as part of their Europe-wide perambulations, and who continued to appear in the music halls and circuses and on the international circuit. Their Scottish counterparts also toured widely. Of those listed above as born in Scotland, Babette and Raoul appeared in Bombay, Delhi and Paris; Jack Francois was born into a touring comedy act (for whom Edinburgh was probably just a stopover) and made his stage debut at the Walhalla Theatre, Berlin; Billy Crotchett took his multi-instrumental act (including piano, bagpipe, spoons and musical saw) around the world as part of Scottish shows and as far afield as Japan as a solo turn; Jack Melville toured America, Germany, France and Italy; The Mysterious Mysticus toured widely in North America and appeared in circus in India and the Far East; while Younger and Younger featured in theatres in Germany, Austria, France, Italy, Hungary and Scandinavia. Having international experience was an important credential for these acts. George Johnstone recalls a 'Hungarian' strongman with an assistant 'spieling' for him as if he could not speak English. When George had a chat with him at the end of the week, the strongman asked him, 'Where d'ye come fae, Mac?' – the 'Hungarian' was from Greenock.

SPECIALITY DANCERS
BABETTE & RAOUL

Formed after the World War II, husband and wife act Babette and Raoul
specialised in slow 'adagio' dancing and lifting. Their greatest success was
with their 'jungle fantasy': Babette dressed as a snake is lured by
Raoul the snake charmer down a 21-foot rope. He loses his flute in
a flash of thunder, they have a fight and the act ends with her being flung
half the length of the stage and landing in the splits.

One of the outstanding nineteenth-century Scottish entertainers, John Henry Anderson, spent much of his career travelling the world and claimed to have appeared before all the crowned heads of Europe; as well as King Kammehameha of the Sandwich Islands, Pomare Queen of the Society Islands and Paul Chief of the Canadian Indians. A farmer's son from Deeside bitten by the theatrical bug, he joined a touring show in his teens when his parents died. His attempt at acting failed and he went to work for Aberdeen showman Big Scottie who had a magician's booth, learned the business and married the showman's daughter. Aged 17 he set out on his own with such success across Britain that by 1840 he was calling himself the 'Wizard of the North'. In 1845 he borrowed nearly £15,000 and opened his own wooden City Theatre in Glasgow (credited as a significant turning point in the gradually improving status of professional conjurors). After four months it burned to the ground and Anderson set off on a national and European tour to clear his debts. Another fire at London's Covent Garden Theatre in 1855 saw him on tour again to Australia and North America. By 1862 he was back in Scotland, appearing in the new music-hall venues, dying aged 59 in 1874.

Performers like Anderson followed in the footsteps of the touring medicine and alchemical shows with entertainers that had lured the crowds in Scotland since at least the Middle Ages. One of the most famous of the seventeenth-century showman-quacks, Doctor John Pontus, is recorded as having made three tours of Scotland, in 1633, 1643 and 1662-63. As John Lamont recorded in his *Diary*:

> *Every tyme he had his publicke stage erected, and sold theron droggs to the peopell .... Each tyme he had his peopell that played on the scaffold, ane ay playing the foole, and ane other by leaping and dancing on the rope, etc ....*

The association between science, magic and medicine is an ancient one (among the laws attributed to King Kenneth was an ordinance that jugglers, wizards and necromancers and those who engaged the help of spirits should be burnt to death), but by the nineteenth century, as medicine became more scientific, showmen like Anderson reflected this. They continued to exploit the 'mysterious' zone between science and magic, but presented a more 'scientific', educative face. Anderson disingenuously billed an 1848 show in Glasgow where he sent a child to sleep with chloroform as one of his 'Feats of NATURAL MAGIC, illustrative of the fallacy of DEMONOLOGY AND WITCHCRAFT', precisely to sensationalise this 'wonder of modern Science' (the first operation under anaesthetic was performed in 1846).

Continuing in this vein, Anderson's fellow Deesider Sam Murphy, better known as Dr Walford Bodie, illusionist, ventriloquist and conjuror, was perhaps best known for 'scientific' spectaculars involving such stunts as hypnotising a volunteer into a week-long trance and, more commonly, passing thousands of volts through victims in a shower of sparks. (His heyday around the turn of the century was a time of rapid scientific innovation involving electricity.) Like generations of his predecessors, he fell foul of the medical profession with his spurious title and many alleged cures. One Leith resident remembered crutches hanging Lourdes-like outside the Gaiety 'as proof of his supposed cures'. Claims and counter-claims for the medical efficacy for his 'bloodless surgery' generated valuable publicity and Bodie toured widely, topping bills at the turn of the century. Even in the more knowing period of the 1920s and '30s, he ran his own long roadshow tours around Scotland.

By the 1950s his type of big touring magic show was on the decline everywhere, but Falkirk showman Dave Hunter embarked on a scaled-down venture after finishing a long partnership running his own revues. He decided 'there hasn't been a good hypnotist goin up the North o Scotland', contacted Scottish magician John Barrington, and proposed a tour where he would present Barrington as just over from America on a fishing holiday:

A very good-lookin lad, very good. And I got him dressed to perfection. When he walked on that stage …. 'Ooooh! Here's something', because I told them 'Ladies and Gentlemen, tonight we have with us the world's greatest hypnotist … just over here and taking a run through the north of Scotland … ladies and gentlemen, here is John Barrington'. And when he walked out you could see the movement in their seats. And so he started and it was a great success …. 'Oh, go and see Barrington if he comes here', you know. So we had a very good run at that ….

As Dave himself put it, it was some time since there had been a good hypnotist touring the north, and his tour was probably one of the last before television made even far-flung rural audiences harder to thrill. More recently, however, illusionists and hypnotists have managed to re-invent themselves for new audiences, packing city-centre theatres. As for quack medicine shows, the more exotic fringes of the alternative health boom continue to embody the age-old alliance of magic, medicine and show.

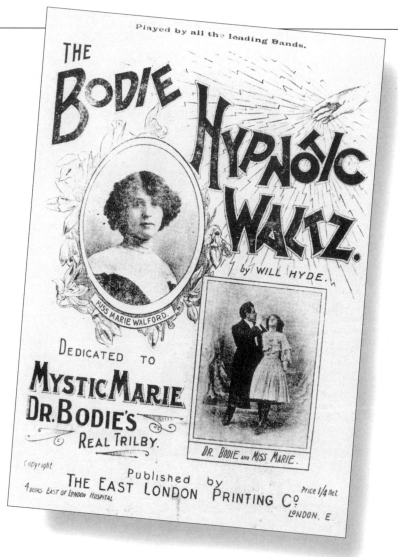

'Dr' Walford Bodie knew how to catch the
public imagination. Mystic Marie was his pianist sister.

Davie Brown, a wine and spirit merchant turned proprietor and manager of
the long-running Royal Music Hall in Glasgow's Dunlop Street. (*Bailie*)

BACKSTAGE AND FRONT OF HOUSE

… is the electrician about? (Asks posh turn newly arrived in the theatre)
No-one called Alec about here. (Replies Stage-cleaner)
I mean the man that looks after the lights.
Oh, that's Wullie.
And who's the stage manager?
That's Wullie
Then who's the manager?
That's Wullie…
… When does the Orchestra arrive?
Oh, she disnae come doon in the mornin, unless its anythin important ….

HARRY GORDON and JACK HOLDEN in *THE STAGE CLEANER*

Free and easies and the early music halls required few staff. Proprietors did much of the booking, auditioning, managing, and on occasion wielding the chairman's hammer or even performing. They became local celebrities and there was strong identification between proprietor, theatre and audience, with many venues being known by the name of the owner or lessee: 'Frame's Royal Music Hall', 'Shearer's Whitebait' or 'Davie Broon's'. But as matters became more business-like this changed, as suggested by the *Bailie* magazine (July 1873) profile of Davie Broon:

He does not now preside in person, nor take a part
as he once could with great effect in the fine old glees

we hear in these days so rarely, but he still keeps 'the master's eye' on all that goes on with excellent effect. For a generation at least his name has been 'familiar in the mouth' of everybody in the West of Scotland who indulges, or indulged, in a little relaxation o' nights.

Proprietors like the Woolley brothers at Greenock Empire, Alex Frutin at the Glasgow Metropole, or the Portobello Pavilion's André Letta with his trademark button-hole carnation, were much involved in what went on in their theatres and were well known to patrons. A E Pickard, whose extensive Glasgow property portfolio included the Panopticon (formerly the Britannia Music Hall), was reputed to stand by the side of the stage on first nights and use a large pole with a hook on the end to yank off performers who failed to please, and pelt over-rowdy members of the audience with screw nails from the top of a ladder by the side of the stage.

In most cases, however, theatres were owned by limited companies, or businessmen like George Urie Scott (who owned a chain of small cinemas on the south side of Glasgow, the Palais Dennistoun dance-hall, as well as the Glasgow Pavilion and Empress theatres). It was the theatre manager who dealt with the public, waiting to greet regulars at the front door. Managers like kilted Claude Worth of the Leith Gaiety, or the

Edinburgh Theatre Royal's 'Bumper' Wark in immaculate top hat and tails, bow-tie and waxed moustache, became local characters. A dinner jacket was more usual and according to Mac Fyfe, former assistant manager to Glasgow Empress manager Jack Worth (brother of Claude), he was entitled to a new suit every two years.

Meeting and greeting was an important part of the whole theatre-going ritual and to this extent theatre managers, who were occasionally ex-performers themselves, stood halfway between public, performance and proprietor. In some cases, usually in smaller theatres, the role of manager and producer was combined, as in the case of Claude Worth (formerly a light comedian and pantomime dame) at the Leith Gaiety, or Roy Don (who was previously an all-rounder in the Bouncing Dillons) who looked after the Edinburgh Palladium for the Younger family, acting as manager, licensee and producer.

More usually, as in the theatres owned or controlled by Galts, managers acted as on-the-spot administrators. Given their local knowledge they advise on what might work in different theatres. Archie Foley remembers his father Andrew (who managed the Aberdeen Tivoli and Edinburgh Palladium) going off with other Galt's employees to assess acts in other theatres, having regular strategy meetings at their Glasgow head offices, enforcing contracts (making a reluctant

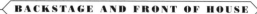

'Glimpses behind the scenes', 1882. (*Quiz*)

Telephone : 27107.
Telegrams : "Proscenium, Edinburgh."

William Mutrie & Son Ltd
Established 1847.

The Outstanding Costumiers & Scenic Contractors

PROUDLY ANNOUNCE THE ACQUISITION
OF NEW AND EXTENSIVE PREMISES AT

Proscenium House, 32-34 Hamilton Place,
EDINBURGH 3

Complete Wardrobes and Settings as supplied to principal Theatres,
for Opera, Musical Comedy Drama, Pageant, Pantomime, etc.

We Cater Specially for All Amateur Operatic Productions

FULL PRODUCTIONS STAGED—LARGE OR SMALL
ALL ESTIMATES GRATIS

The Largest Stock of Wigs, Costumes & Scenery outside London

Irish act go on stage and mouth the national anthem at the end of a show) and advising on such local peculiarities as the length of material to be sewn on chorus girls briefs when they played in Aberdeen. In general, however, what happened on stage was left to the producers who came as part of touring or resident shows.

The manager and his assistant were in overall charge of the theatre staff, which in general consisted of the minimum of full-time employees, the bulk of staff coming in as part-time staff paid on a 'performance' rate agreed with their trade union, NATKE (National Association of Theatrical and Kine Employees). Both part and full-time staff were members of this union (originally formed as the United Kingdom Theatrical and Music Hall Stage Employees in 1890), and although wages and conditions left much to be desired, industrial disputes were relatively rare, most part-timers glad of the work. Managers, however, did not belong to any union, and Mac Fyfe remembers arguing with George

Urie Scott over a rise of ten shillings (his weekly wage was £6. 10s.).

Typically the front-of-house team included box-office, cloakroom and bar staff, usherettes (usually two to a level), and perhaps two or three 'day-men' who would clean in the morning and come in the evenings to check tickets (or in the case of the inevitably rowdy Friday night second house, three or four men to handle any bother). The manager or his assistant dealt with wages and tax returns, oversaw advance reservations, checked accounts, and if bookings were thin for a Monday night first house, would issue free tickets to staff and local hospitals to 'paper the house'. While the second house was running they cashed up the takings from tickets, programmes, ices, cloakrooms and, of course, the bars, in time to get the money deposited into the nearest night safe.

Not surprising, given their common ancestry, the links between showbusiness and the licensed trade were strong. The variety business increasingly depended on theatre bars for revenue and many pubs publicised their theatre-land location, displayed bills, kept copies of the various theatrical papers and boasted of the artistes who visited. Comedian Jock Mills (who ran his own pub in his retirement) probably spoke for the whole of showbusiness in his song 'Carrie Nation', which was recorded in response to the 1908 visit of American temperance campaigner Mrs Carrie Nation (whose own 'The Last Pub' was a very popular music-hall item, recorded several times):

Oh, Carrie, I think you're slightly gone …
It's madness you could think,
we can do without our drink,
Carrie you will have to stop your carry on.

Regarding her threat that 'every man she meets with a glass to his mouth, she will knock it from his hand', Mills gleefully comments, 'I would like to see her in the Coocaddens on a Saturday night closin time, and a navvy finishin his last pint' (the Cowcaddens was a heavily populated working-class district with a disproportionate number of Glasgow's pubs).

In the years after World War II the bar's importance increased as the pinch was felt in the box-office. The Empress, for example, went from two to three bars, and in 1954 when business began to lag at the Greenock Empire, the Woolley brothers built a brand new bar, reckoned, when they closed in 1957, to be the only profit-making part of the whole venture. Singer George Johnstone remembers being dressed down by Metropole proprietor Alex Frutin for running a minute over time: 'You'll take it out. One minute per house is two minutes per night. It's twelve minutes per week. Do you know how much whiskey I can sell in twelve minutes?'

Preparing a backdrop. (Scottish Life Archive)

Backstage, the staff comprised a permanent stage-manager and assistant, chief electrician/ lighting engineer, full-time stage crew, and, depending on the scale of production, perhaps half a dozen 'performance' staff who would also have day jobs elsewhere. The theatre manager was in overall charge, but backstage was left under the control of the stage manager. Given the quick-fire nature of variety, both in terms of the weekly 'get-ins' of new performers and props and the many changes of act during shows, back-stage was an area of work needing skilled co-ordination to keep things running smoothly (scene changes, for example, were pared down to under a minute).

Variety theatres tended not to employ wardrobe mistresses or scenery designers: a stock of 20 or 30 all-purpose cloths was kept to cover most possibilities, with any additional scenery being produced by in-house stagehands. Touring shows might bring their own minimal cloths and the occasional, particularly English, solo acts might bring their own. Mac Fyfe recalls veteran English 'speciality' comedian Bob Nelson have his cloth go up in flames when subjected to the regular Monday morning blowtorch test by the fire safety officer. In the case of Howard and Wyndham, however, with their rolling programmes of five or more pantomimes and lavish summer shows, the company had its own large team of staff, including production managers, wardrobe mistresses, set designers, electricians and carpenters to look after the great numbers of costumes, props, scenery and equipment which had to be moved from one theatre to the next.

For regular, twice-nightly variety theatres, any special costumes and props were hired from theatrical suppliers and were the responsibility of the stage manager. Much of the Scottish variety business was supplied by William Mutries in Edinburgh, a long-running theatrical suppliers established in 1847 and taken over by former actor turned producer Fraser Neal in 1935. In 1952 Mutries had 750 hampers in use, a staff of 100, and a hefty weekly laundry bill; easy to believe given how often their name crops up in pros' reminiscences. Baskets of Mutries props travelled to all the seaside and city-centre variety shows during the summer, with bursts of business in November when pantomime costumes were dispatched and in March when they returned.

Also under the manager, but largely left under the control of the musical director, was the theatre orchestra. Writing about the start of his career in the 1850s, Glasgow violinist Carl Volti (Archibald Milligan) notes that with few venues employing permanent musicians, visiting musicians found little work in Glasgow: 'His visit was generally of brief duration, as he would soon have starved.' Apart from the old Theatre Royal, Volti mentions only Parry's geggie with a

band of three, and the Jupiter Saloon:'I was never in it, but I understand that it was a kind of "free-and-easy", and they had a band of one – a fiddler.' He probably underestimates the number of musicians playing, yet there is no doubt that with the opening of music halls opportunities multiplied:'These all employed good bands, and so professional musicians were brought to the city.' Music halls made much of their bands as an element of refinement and the Edinburgh New Alhambra, in its 1862 opening publicity, was not alone amongst the early wave of new venues in listing the players in its ten-piece orchestra by name. (Bryce's 'free and easy', by contrast, made do with a pianist and violinist.)

Few details survive of these theatre musicians, but amongst the best known of them were the pianist-accompanists like J C Booth. He came from Congleton in Cheshire, started his career in London, and by 1887 was working at the Royal Music Hall in Glasgow, becoming musical director, manager and agent in advance for W F Frame's concert party, as well as author of popular Scotch songs for tenors J W Bowie and J M Hamilton. Latterly he established his own 'Booth's Orchestra', dressed in blue uniforms with red facings, which was available for balls and functions, including the St Andrew's Hall concerts organised by Walter Freer. In Freer's opinion a good accompanist was 'the essential feature' and

'James Booth was the most helpful accompanist of my time. Every artiste loved him. He was a happy, jolly man, with none of the peevishness and tantrums that afflicted so many performers'.

Between the wars there was a boom in live music. As well as theatres employing dozens of musicians, there were the numerous smaller seaside and concert party venues with one or two musicians, cinema orchestras and pianists, *palais de dance* bands, and numerous other tea-dance musicians playing in cafés and arcades. Theatre musicians, however, remained a breed apart, more professionalised and organised since the formation of the musicians union (founded in 1893 as the Amalgamated Musicians Union). This, according to Edinburgh dance-band bassist and saxophonist Al Stewart, was really a 'theatre musicians union' (the more semi-professional jazz and dance-band musicians stayed away). As such, though wages for theatre musicians might not be any better than for dance-band players, there was stricter control over conditions, especially hours worked, with overtime charged by the quarter hour. As a result, though there was give and take between management and musicians, if the shop steward was so inclined then relations could be fraught.

Combined with the quick-change nature of the variety theatre business, this meant that there was little time for rehearsal. Drummer Frank

Duffy remembers having perhaps just a morning's rehearsal for a variety show, a day's rehearsal for a long-running pantomime, or, in the case of the King's pantomime, two days 'because it was such an important show'. Theatre orchestra musicians had to be 'very, very good readers', able to play the music at first sight. Edinburgh dance-band pianist Arthur Allan did not play in variety theatre orchestras because it was 'a very advanced kind of work' (even though he had toured the Moss Empire circuit in a showband, topping the bill at the London Palladium in 1926 in 'Mark Reiver and his Scottish Revellers' and worked in pantomime and summer show rehearsals at the King's Theatre):

> They went in on a Monday morning, and along the front of the stage would be the books for the act. You didn't know what you were going to be playing. You could be playing ragtime, you could be playing ballads, you could be playing operatic. These men were all skilled, and yet they were being paid a few pounds a week. Great players, able, as I say, to look at what's in front of you and play it.

Bobby Dowds, a long-serving musical director at various theatres including the Glasgow Empire, was highly regarded for his musical skill, being able at short notice to provide full transcriptions for the instrumentalists in the orchestra from

Joe Smith and his band, Leith Alhambra, 1925. Note the doubling on
instruments (cello/brass and violin/banjo) and presence of saxophones
enabling the band to play the wide range of music from Scottish to
Jazz which theatre work demanded.

piano scores supplied by visiting headlining singers. At the other end of the spectrum in the Aberdeen Beach Pavilion, the music was provided by resident pianist Alice Stephenson (many resident pianists were women) whose highly accomplished novelty and jazz playing can be heard on some of the many recordings made by Harry Gordon in the 1930s.

Given that music was so important, with the orchestra busy for much of the show, it is no surprise to find the decline of variety-theatre orchestras often cited both as a symptom and cause of the general decline of the business. Between the wars the main city-centre variety theatres employed orchestras of between eight and 14 musicians, but as the decline set in many orchestras were cut back to four or five, and in the smaller venues to a pianist or latterly an organist. At the Greenock Empire the orchestra was reduced from nine to five, and thereafter called 'the band'.

Moxon Girls outside Cragburn Pavilion (*May Morrison at the left,
see page 108*). Note the costumes, no doubt of the type
May remembered having to spend much of her time off altering.

WORK AND PLAY

Showbusiness was often the family business. Dynasties of performers, agents and impresarios that stretched back three or four generations were common, and marrying within the business virtually the norm (notably husband and wife double acts). This gave a certain stability and continuity to what was otherwise a fickle and uncertain life.

Those who did not come from showbusiness backgrounds could face family disapproval; showpeople still had the taint of immorality and many a parent worried about the sort of life their children might be getting into. One talented Leith boy was recruited by producers Levi & Co (who had placed adverts in the local papers and held auditions for new talent which they then packaged in a touring show of 'discoveries' around the country). He spent over seven years in the business as part of a dancing double act in pantomime and variety around the country (for ten shillings a week), but at the age of 16 had to come home. As his brother remembered:

> He enjoyed it very much, but it eventually came that my mother, who was a wee bit of a prude – which people were at that sort o time – about the theatre, thought that it was time he was away from it, because he was gettin tae the age where he was perhaps seein more than he should. So I think he would be about sixteen when she made him come home, and then he started to work as an office boy in Wordies, the contractors in Leith.

Though George Clarkson had already been on the stage by the age of eleven, his parents would not let him turn professional when he left school, wanting him to get a 'proper' trade. They made him spend 'five year's agony as a french polisher':

… I was just counting the days and counting the weeks till my five years was up and I only got one week of journeyman's wages when I said to ma father, I said 'I'm off to the stage', so he said 'Well don't put away your brushes and don't put away anything because … you'll be back in a fortnight's time and you'll need them again'.

As it turned out, Clarkson went on to work for 50 years as a dancer and producer.

In the lean years of the 1920s and '30s, a career in variety became very appealing, ensuring a steady stream of hopefuls for the regular talent shows in theatres that always drew lively, if not supportive, audiences. Bill McLenaghan, later to work as chauffeur to comedian Dave Willis, recalled one such turn at Pringles Palace:

I remember an act getting booed off, and it was breakin her heart, and that was my mother, her debut. She was getting her audition, and instead of havin the audition wi a producer and the wee lights, and the cleaner at the back wi a fag in her hand, it was a live audience. And I was down there wi my granny, and I remember my granny sayin 'don't move just now, we'll go out, when the next act goes on we'll go out ….'

The other route for aspiring stars was the lively network of amateur and semi-professional engagements. Cinemas and theatres closed on Sundays, and many burgh and church halls staged rudimentary variety concerts: no scenery or back cloths, with a pianist or at most a couple of musicians. Numerous amateurs plied the concert party networks of local halls, never giving up their day jobs. Inverness physical training instructor Donald Dallas was a popular figure in singer Lee Fraser's concert party, with a wide repertoire of often quite radical local songs such as 'Bonny Black Isle' ('I've been in the model, the puirhoose, the jile, but none can come up to the bloomin Black Isle ….') and 'There was a Man' (sung to a psalm tune and poking fun at the 'Wee Frees').

Many amateurs hoped to become professional. Like many comedians, Glaswegian Jack Friell progressed from amateur dramatics at the local parochial hall. As his son put it: 'He was a hard working young married man with prospects [with Scottish Legal Assurance] until he got the theatre bug ….' Taking the stage name 'Jack Delmore', he formed a trio, acting as straightman to comedian (and tailor by trade) Eck Rae, and getting bookings through Galts around the smaller halls. When Rae left the stage to return to tailoring, Friell continued to work as a feed to various comics, but by the mid '30s 'his engagements came at bigger and bigger intervals, and he was working as a salesman going door to door'. His story is typical of the acts who tried to make it in the local Scottish scene. They haunted 'Poverty Corner' (a spot at the junction of Renfield Street and Sauchiehall Street, near the appropriately named Lauder's bar and within site of Galt's and Collins' agencies) where they were visited by small-time variety agents and promoters in search of performers. As script-writer Alex Mitchell recalled: 'These homespun entrepreneurs knew the regulars who would wait there in the hope of a proposition such as, "It's a couple of pounds for the night, your tea and a lift in the lorry to Falkirk and back".'

The scarcity of professional acts during World War II opened up more opportunities. Springburn joiner Harry Shaw, who had played in a twelve-man concert party around the local public halls and charity concerts, found profes-sional engagements when he was taken on by an agent with his 'Novelty Comedy' double act 'Spring and Burn', and appeared in Glasgow's Empire, Empress and Queen's, as well as in Dundee and Motherwell. Outside the war years, however, even experienced professional acts had to settle for filling their date books piecemeal, a highly competitive process with artistes subject to constant assessment. Propri-etors and managers kept written notes in the margins of pay books about how acts had gone down, and agents depended on being able to judge who would (or would not) go where. Galts kept an alphabetical 'Report Book' giving descriptions of acts: 'Very good trick cyclists. Opened crinoline and gent in court dress. Then into old-fashioned polka dresses and finished modern with gent balancing girl on fit-up attached to shoulders while girl on revolving bar. Good act for variety ...'. It also listed appraisals of how 'useful' they might be: 'Thought she was rather common, but evidently that's how they want it. Getting a lot of money'; 'Very pleasing and bookable'; 'Practically beginners'; 'Good punch act'; 'Dreadful.'

Not surprisingly, relationships between agents, management and performers, though dependent on each other, were often strained. The many in-jokes about agents reflected this. Comedy musical act Billy Crockett told me a story about an agent coming out of his office: a Scotch comic down on his luck collapses in the gutter, the agent comes over, lifts the comic's head on his knee, fans his face and tells the crowd, 'Stand back, stand back. Let him have air'. Suddenly the comic revives and asks, 'What about Dundee and Inverness?'

Comedian Bobby Telford's drawn-out fight with Galts, who felt entitled to take a percentage on performances which he had arranged independently, was typical of many disputes that resulted in litigation.

Relationships had been tense ever since the business had become more professionalised in the late-nineteenth century. This led ultimately to the music-hall strikes of 1906-7 (a London-based struggle between over-powerful theatre syndicates and over-exploited performers, which spread to the provinces). Although this led to the formation in 1906 of the Variety Artistes' Federation (VAF) bringing all ranks of performer together, agents and managers remained powerful. For chorus girls in particular, conditions were poor: shoddy dressing-rooms up in the gods (which meant running up and down two or three flights of stairs between changes), no showers (having to wash down in sinks), spending weekends washing, starching and altering ill-fitting hampers of costumes, not being paid for rehearsal time, and with no paid holiday. But as May Morrison recalled, with her employer May Moxon as a head figure in the VAF, there was little they could do about it. She recalls a visit backstage from Equity representative Dick Barton during the 1955 Metropole summer season, telling them about the advantages of joining Equity:

And it sounded too good to be true, because up until then we had to do what we were told … I never remember any girl ever saying 'no', 'cannae do it', 'We want such and …', sueing or anything: nothing like that. So we all agreed that this would be great. The next thing, Miss Moxon was down like a ton of bricks on top of us, with pieces of paper which we had to sign. There were ten of us in the Metropole. I take it that she'd go round all the other places … and she says 'and you'll all sign these pieces of paper'. And on it, if I remember correctly, it was to the effect that we wouldn't join Equity …. And, of course, what did we do but sign it. I mean we were waiting on getting the boot out the door any minute, which really couldn't happen … who was she going to get to replace us right away?

(When chorus girls did eventually join Equity, wages doubled from £2 to £4.)

There was also a good deal of competition between performers who were as keenly aware of the rankings (who played what sort of venues) as the agents. Comedians in particular bickered about who got the funny lines and were known to have newcomers flung off shows if they proved too amusing. When Tommy Hood, one of Tommy Morgan's feeds, decided to go solo in his own show, he received a legal document at half-past five on the Monday evening before the first house, stating that if he used any of Morgan's material he would be sued (a difficult point to prove either way considering that most sketches were really re-workings from a common stock).

Jealousies were fuelled by often huge wage

differentials. An international performer like Harry Lauder commanded a weekly salary of £1500, and comedians topping the Scottish number ones and twos might earn up to £300 in the 1930s, rising to £500 with a percentage of the takings in the 1950s. The comedian's feed (as often as not a frustrated comedian) could be on a tenth of this. Nevertheless, wages for even the humblest of acts were a great improvement on the average working wages. George Clarkson's five pounds a week at the start of his stage career was several times the 15 shillings he earned as a journeyman french polisher, and wages overall had improved decade by decade.

According to 'Old Growler' in his 1895 article 'Reminiscences of the Glasgow Music Halls', when he first went to the halls in the 1870s comic singers 'didn't strut the streets in fur trimmed coats, or show a vast expanse of shirt front, with a diamond decoration…. Long engagements and short salaries were the order of the day'. Local star W G Ross had 18 months at the Britannia for £5 a week. By 1895 wages had increased and a Scotch comedian was getting £10. 10s:

The price list of the local pros is a study for the uninitiated. Artistes of extraordinary abilities demand from three to five guineas for a concert in the city. Artistes of ordinary abilities are content with a couple of guineas, and artistes of no abilities vary in value from £5 down to 5s.

By the inter-war years, the minimum wage was the £2 earned by chorus girls, and the typical salary for most singers, musical and speciality acts was between £15 and £30 a week.

Whatever the case, for the majority of pros wages were soon eaten up by periods of 'rest', and when working it was consumed by the extra expenses of the lifestyle. Performers were always touring, and although their own travelling expenses might be paid for, those of their families were not. Children had to be farmed out to relatives or sent to boarding school, digs had to be paid for, and many would send a portion of their earnings home to their parents. Most chorus girls had just a few shillings left over at the end of a week, and this would depend on being able to share digs. May Morrison recalled having four or five to a bed:

That sounds ridiculous, but it's true. That happened at Dunfermline, to get it cheap. To get digs for thirty shillings or twenty-five shillings you shared a bed with four. And see if you were small like me, you were stuck in the middle.

Top turns stayed in the best local hotel, but most pros rang ahead to theatres which kept lists of the theatrical landladies who were well known in the business. Their foibles formed the subject matter of many an anecdote, usually along the lines of the following excerpt from Harry Gordon and Jack Holden's sketch 'The Stage Cleaner':

> *I say, where can I get apartments round here?*
> *Oh, Margaret, where can this gentleman find*
> *   some apartments round here?*
> *Come on, tell me.*
> *Oh, I say, just imagine a beautiful room with a*
> *   great big fireplace, electric lights, ham and eggs*
> *   for breakfast, four course lunch, and a hot*
> *   supper, all in for thirteen bob a week.*
> *Splendid, where is this place?*
> *Oh, I dinna ken, but just imagine!*

Though most of the stories about theatrical landladies focus on the mean, eccentric or poverty-stricken, they were generally well liked and took good care of their 'theatricals', making sure there was a hot meal waiting for them when they got home late at night. In exchange they were often given complimentary tickets for performances.

Stories about unusual theatrical digs, like jokes about agents, and the many tales of mishaps and accidents, were part of an extensive theatrical lore addressing the stresses and strains

of the business. It helped to bind performers together as 'real pros', enabling them to conjure up a sense of a working community in venue after venue. In this lore was embodied a picture of the business that tended to smooth over and soften its edges. Stories of on-stage disasters were particularly common. A good many involved drunken antics onstage, with performers having to have a 'stiffener' before being able to perform; or the usually unsuccessful attempts of managers and producers to keep well-known drinkers dry. The lifestyle was highly conducive to heavy drinking; performers were away from home, at a loose end during the daytime when not rehearsing, subject to pre-performance nerves, and there was a well-established tradition of 'stars' being expected to display hospitality as part of their larger-than-life personae. Stories about alcoholic pros, like stories of scenery falling apart and sketches misfiring, dealt with real aspects of the life, but offered catharsis in the telling. The drunk was sobered up, and the disaster was averted at the last minute.

Likewise, stories of cameraderie and mutual aid crop up in performers' reminiscences to an extent that seems as much rose-tinted memory (given the jealousies, competitiveness and hierarchies) as reality. The reality was largely informal; established pros giving newcomers a leg up, lending money, or giving a room to a colleague who was ill or down on their luck, or just swapping the stories and gossip that gave the business a sense of common purpose. It could take a more organised form; many male Victorian pros were Masons (guaranteeing plenty of one-night stands at Masonic functions if nothing else). Though it does not seem to have played as much of a role in forming professional identity as other trades unions, there was the Variety Artistes' Federation (VAF) and the Show Business Benevolent Fund (SBBF) (Scotland), established in 1895 as the Scottish Musical Artistes Benevolent Fund (incorporating comedian W F Frame and music publisher Mozart Allan's Benevolent Funds), the oldest such charitable organisation in Britain. The SBBF continues to give financial support and arrange holidays for retired pros, an important function for those not in a position to retire and open a hotel (the popular, if occasionally disastrous, choice for many Scottish comedians) but who ended their careers in the business with few outside resources to fall back on.

For most, the business was their life and their home. The rivalries, anti-social hours, damp dressing rooms (usually furnished with the rats that are a recurring motif in theatre-lore) were, for many, worth it. It was not so much for the thrill of being on stage (although this was undoubtedly important), but because, as May Morrison put it, 'it was a lovely business to be in because most of them were lovely people ... we were appreciated because we worked hard'. Or, as Dave Hunter remembered after 40 years out of the business working as a car salesman:

We were in different towns every week and everything was fresh again, fresh again and the old theatre people they were marvellous people. I loved every one of them; they were always 'if we met here and there' there was always a good hand out to say 'Hello' and 'It's nice to see ye'.

The official journal of the Variety Artistes Federation, *The Performer*, was eagerly scanned every week by pros north and south of the Border for all the latest jobs and gossip.

Week Commencing Monday, 18th September, 1939.

"Suicide Sal & her Gang"

:: REVUE. ::

1 OPENING—SUICIDE SAL & HER GANG.
2 JIMMY REID—Bright & Breezy.
3 TONNETTS—Scotch Medley.
4 SKIT—"The Anniversary"
5 JACKSON SISTERS—Sell Sunshine.
6 IRISH SCENA—Billy Fields & Co.
7 GEORGE VALENTE—The Music Box.
8 IVY VAL—Pep & Personality.
9 SKIT—"The Black-out"
10 JACK CARR—"We are the Boys"
11 JACKSON SISTERS—Modern Misses.
12 PARTY SKETCH—Billy Fields & Co.
13 JIMMY REID—Yin o' yer ain.
14 FRANK & DORIS DROY—Themselves.
15 DANCE HALL—The Company.

GOD SAVE THE KING.

SPECIAL NOTICE—This Programme is subject to alteration if necessity may occasion, and the Management disclaim responsibility for the non-appearance of any Artist.

All Classes of Repairs completed by Experts

A programme for Paisley Theatre, marked with detailed timings for turns.
Pros had to hone their appearances almost to the second, to keep the
houses running on time. (*See pp 116-117 for 'Suicide Sal' tour*).

'YIN O' YER AIN'

According to journalist Colm Brogan, writing in 1938, Scottish comedians fell into two categories: 'pastoral' old-fashioned performers who were 'more or less divorced from reality'; and 'industrial' younger comics who were 'nearer the bone' and in closer touch with audiences. Brogan's distinction is a useful starting point but a little too neat.

Although most of the popular comedians who came into the business after World War I were from working-class backgrounds, not all of them – despite the lingering myth – were 'industrial' graduates schooled in the macho banter of the factory floor. Tommy Morgan reluctantly worked as a shipyard plater's helper, and Dave Willis as an engineer. Tommy Lorne, however, had worked for a hairdresser, George West was a lawyer's clerk, and Bobby Telford was private secretary to a Lord Provost. Summer season comic Dave Bruce came from a well-off business family, went to Allen Glen's school, and was a draughtsman at Harland and Wolff before turning professional in the 1920s with partner (ex-miner) Jack Radcliffe; whereas Jack Anthony came from a showbusiness family.

Ayrshire coast summer season favourite Dave Bruce in Hollywood mode. He was noted for his ability, as one reviewer wrote, to 'vary from homely Scots humour to something approaching cultured wit', and was one of only a few Scottish comedians to work in England.

While male comedians tended to get the billings and made sure of the best laughs, there were many well-loved comediennes or, as they were known, 'comedy women': Sylvia Watt, for example, was a pantomime favourite with hallmark white make-up; there was soubrette Mae Wynne, and also the comedy duo 'wives' such as Grace Clark, Doris Droy and Dora Lindsay, who played for laughs against straight-men husbands.

Whatever their backgrounds, however, comedians knew their business. They knew that audiences wanted some reflection of their 'industrial' lives, plenty of up-to-date, outward-looking topicality, but also a good dose of old-fashioned sentiment and nostalgia for which they remained indebted to the 'pastoral' tradition.

Among the 'pastoral' comics, Brogan ranked Dundonian Will Fyffe after Lauder. Fyffe gained success across Britain and abroad from the 1920s with song and patter character studies similar to Lauder's. But Fyffe came from a different background. He was a character actor, graduate of the Rob Roy 'national drama' tradition since working from the age of twelve in his father's 'fit-up' (portable theatre), and he developed a career in films in the 1930s alongside his variety and pantomime work. Likewise, Lauder's Greenock contemporary Neil Kenyon went

from drama and pantomime in travelling shows to develop a music-hall sketch act of couthy cameos set in the fictitious village of Dunrobin. With this act he toured around Britain for 20 years, also appearing in plays and early silent films.

This sentimental, nostalgic 'character study' strand in comedy was directly taken up by variety comedians like Jack Radcliffe and Alec Finlay (billed as the 'Pocket Lauder'). However, it was an element in the work of all types of Scottish comedian in the countless sketches about doctors, postmen, ministers and other assorted worthies in fictional, sub-kailyard 'villages', and more generally in the evocation of a sense of close urban community, that was a crucial ingredient in comedy routines. It continues to colour television manifestations of Scottish comedy as in the popular soap 'High Road' (set in yet another fictional village) and in figures like Rab C Nesbitt (the dystopian off-spring of generations of stage drunks).

As well as drawing on the Scotch comic heritage, variety era comedians were keenly attuned to popular culture at large. George West was an avid film fan, specialising in parodies of stars like Shirley Temple, WC Fields, Mae West and, with partner Jack Raymond, Laurel and Hardy. Scottish sketch artists were quick to adopt the quick-fire cross-patter of English and

American comedy and to produce home-grown versions of the new styles of comic song. This can be seen in song parodies which reflected the widening range of influences to which audiences were exposed and played this off against more prosaic subject matter and established types of performance. Popular Aberdeen-based Harry Gordon's 'Drambuie Blues' starts off as an old-fashioned music-hall song informing listeners how boring he finds being teetotal, until half-way through when it switches to a 'bluesy' refrain: 'Oh, I've got the dram, I've got the dram, drambuie blues …', followed by a typical 'drunk' patter. More up-to-date is his 'In the Simmertime', about the Aberdonian holiday-spot of Milltimber:

> [Chorus] *When the coos are mooin to the*
>   *cuckoos,*
> *And the cuckoos are cooin tae the dooes,*
> *When the beezes and the fleazes are yodellin like*
>   *bleezes,*
> *And singin in the treeses the gorgonzolla blues.*
> *Its a peety that ma sweety is so meaty,*
> *She gets sozzled on a single gin and lime.*
> *So now I sit and blether to masel among the*
>   *heather,*
> *In Miltimmer in the simmertime.*

> *I jump on ma scouter*
> *And hit the trail for Couper*
> *To play hockey wi a jockey*
> *Whose so cocky he aye wins.*
> *Then I meet the butcher*
> *Who married Mini the Moucher,*
> *Then I cannon off the cushion*
> *Till I'm pannin ower Torphins,*
> *Back to my log cabin in the pines.*
> *Buddy can ye spare one o yer quines ….*

The song is full of references to Hollywood and consumer exotica, all contained in the framework of fashionable 'log cabin' film songs, with a novelty-Jazz accompaniment by Alice Stevenson, Gordon's resident pianist at the Aberdeen Beach Pavilion. Yet, with its local placenames and rather studied use of dialect, it shows how regional and local identity (not simply Scottish, or even the dominant urban-Glaswegian) remained a vital element in performances.

Songs and sketches were frequently given a localised setting: a well-known landmark, pub, street scene, or the inside of a tenement. Sketches were framed and punctuated with references to neighbourhood events, people's anniversaries, and so on. Comedians, though always remaining in character, routinely broke out of the 'plot' to emphasise the here and now of audience-performance community; responding to hecklers,

Jimmy Nicol. Initially in a double act with his wife, in his solo career the Coatbridge comedian was particularly associated with long summer seasons at the Aberdeen Tivoli.

ad-libbing, using the catchphrases for which they were famous (and which, like Tommy Morgan's 'Clairty, clairty' or Dave Willis'Away up a kye', often had special little histories attached); or, in the case of Charlie Kemble, telling his Rothesay summer season Saturday night audiences, 'See you at Church tomorrow' (most of the cast went to the evening service where the soprano and baritone sang duets for the congregation).

But most influential of all was the role of performers' personae. Frank and Doris Droy's 'Suicide Sal' reworked daringly suggestive (for the time) songs and parodies about man-eating Hollywood femmes-fatales. First Sal declines an 'awfully soft and nancy' fellow, telling him, 'you've got me all wrong, you'd be better to spend the night with old King Kong'. Next she turns down a millionaire with a yacht, and then comes the final verse:

> *Suicide Sal, just a night-club girl;*
> *Once I met a boxer when he was in the ring.*
> *He said 'I'll see you later, you're a pretty little*
> *   thing.'*
> *I said 'I'm Suicide Sal, why everyone calls me pal.'*
> *He thought that he was strong and sturdy,*
> *After I had left him, well, he wasnae*
> *   worth a curdie,*   [small coin]
> *Cos, I'm Sue, just plain Sue, they call me*
> *   Suicide Sal.*

There is little overtly local about this, and the Droys followed the trend for variety and vaudeville husband and wife comedy double acts. However, they were well known as a Glasgow act, strongly identified with the Queen's Theatre and its pantomimes. Remembered as being 'refined' off stage, Doris had a loud, rowdy 'close-mooth' on-stage role. 'Suicide Sal' played this off against a Mae West delivery and the character became notorious, with the 'Suicide Sal and Her Gang' revue touring Scotland in 1939. The character created instant rapport with audiences as they shared in a (then) risqué send-up of the Silver Screen, given the pointedly vernacular climax 'he wasnae worth a curdie'. These 'one of us' personae were honed to perfection by performers. Sammy Murray, principal comedian at the Queen's, for example, sang 'Tiptoe through the Tulips' verbatim, relying for laughs on the absurd contrast with his status as 'Gallus Sammy'.

More elaborate contrasts were possible in the quick-fire song and patter double acts. Martin and Holbein's 'Sally's Sleepy Valley Alley' starts with the orchestra vamping in vaudevillian style, presumably as they sauntered in front of a 'back-court' cloth, before they start singing about their 'ole man river blues', 'Ukelele Lady' and 'Old Parson Jones' with his 'Syncopatin' choir'. The patter continues:

Martin [English accent]: *Oh, by the way Charlie, have you, eh, had your vacation this year?*

Holbein [Scots accent]: *Oh yes, I've travelled extensively – a day here and a day there, mostly here.*

Martin: *Did you travel far?*

Holbein: *Well, I've been as far abroad as Blairgowrie.*

Martin: *Blairgowrie?*

Holbein: *Yes*

Martin: *Indeed?*

Holbein: *No, in jail …. Would you believe it, I can't sleep a wink in Buckingham Palace?*

Martin: *You can't sleep a wink in Buckingham Palace?*

Holbein: *Not a wink.*

Martin: *Why?*

Holbein: *They won't let me.*

Martin: *Well, you can have your palaces, but give me Sally's sleepy Valley Alley.*

[Sing] *We've got neighbours right across the way*
Who holler ragged music till the break of day.
There's a baby and an old man too,
And the cutest little baby there from Honolu lu ….

Being Glaswegian is set off against their Americanised song, with a climax on 'Blairgowrie' where so many working-class Scots went berry-picking; the kind of shared knowledge that bound audience and performer, reinforced in the final celebratory 'you can have your palaces …'. Opposing regional joker and anglicised straight-man (often in the form of posh lawyers and faceless officials who featured in much comedy of the period) was a typical comic strategy, enacting for audiences the confrontation between 'us' and 'them'.

Double acts' patter allowed some scope for dramatic invention within conventional limits, but there was much more scope in sketches. Almost like mini one-act plays, these were the result of a long process of 'theatricalisation' of music-hall acts that had been going on since the 1870s, with duos and trios presenting increasingly elaborate sketches (not strictly legal until changes in theatre licensing laws in the 1900s). *The Performer* published a 1892-93 series of such sketches written by John Alexander and performed by Fanny Wright, Alice Brooks and the McConnell Family: mainly comic arguments between servants, husbands and wives and gossiping neighbours. Alexander's sketches are the same uneven blend of pacy idiom and stodgy moralising found in periodical prose of the time. By the inter-war period these comic sketches, even with the stereotypes and hackneyed gags, had evolved a punchier and rather striking kind of local realism. Glasgow comedian and conjuror

Wullie Lindsay's sketch 'Six home and three away', gives a flavour of this:

  [Cheering]
Straight-man: *The Juniors must have won today.*
Lindsay: *Ach, whit the hell do I care aboot the Juniors, it's the final edition of the Times I want tae see.*
Straight-man: *Ye'r no excited?*
Lindsay: *Not at all, not at all* [delivered as a catch-phrase] *… would you no be excited wi a guid sniff o a coupon comin up …* [newspaper-vendor shouts] *…. Aye, here we are at last.*
Straight-man: *Aye, you don't catch me playin that mug's game.*
Lindsay: *Ach, its only a mug's game when ye lost, and I'm no losin today …* [to vendor] *… hey, final there's yer penny …. Ach, pick the damn thing up yersel.*
Vendor: [moans] *Whit a man!*
Lindsay: *Ah've got ten shillin on the day.*
Straight-man: *Michty God, yer off yer heid!*

Excitement follows as Lindsay finds that his coupon has come up. He goes home promising to buy his wife a coat she has seen at the Co-op shop, but is then furious to find that she has forgotten to take his line to the bookies. Baldly transcribed there is little humour; many such

Glasgow comedian, conjuror and scriptwriter Wullie Lindsay, performing with
the Chinese rings. As well as appearing across Scotland from the 1920s to
the '50s (latterly with a mind-reading act), he also wrote some of
the best songs for top Scottish comedians of the day, usually for little reward.

Scottish performers, especially Harry Lauder, had been making recordings since the 1920s. Between the 1920s and '40s, comedian Harry Gordon made dozens of recordings on Beltona and Parlophone (who also released a number by Wullie Lindsay), the two labels most recorded on by Scottish performers of the variety era.

sketches relied on simply presenting the familiar, if stereotyped, less 'respectable' aspects of life.

Success in this period required a constant flow of new material for the multiple programme changes of summer seasons, and radio and 78 rpm recordings made the shelf-life of many songs and sketches short. Comedians depended on writers like Greenock maths teacher Bill MacDonnell who, according to his own records, between 1941 and 1953 sold a total of 725 items (289 items sold as part-rights – in

other words, material sold at a lower price to several performers; 157 sole rights; and 185 'specials' – material commissioned by established customers; the balance being made up of 'gag set, compere gags, rhymes, rhyme sheets, parodies, medleys, rewrites'). Scriptwriters became adept at concocting in quantity the sort of material that comedians wanted: novel and up-to-date, but with a local, community-oriented dimension.

This can be seen in the scores of recordings

from the 1920s and '30s made by Harry Gordon. Like most performers' sketches, his were often based on the mundane. 'The Washing Day', written and performed with Jack Holden, has two women gossiping in a back-green and mixes a familiar real-life scene, recognisable types, fragments of closely observed colloquial speech and quick-fire cross-talk gags. Typically of such sketches, it is full of cultural contrasts as they discuss, among other things, buying a piano (an emblem of respectability and cultural aspiration) on hire-purchase, a husband's job in the cinema, and playing musical instruments (one plays the mouthie), before ending with an anarchic duet on mouthie and washboard.

Gordon's favourite role was the socially and usually sexually inexperienced 'little fellow' who cannot cope with modern life but somehow gets by and even manages to make fun of it. As with innumerable earlier versions of this gowk figure (J C MacDonald's 'Sandy Saft Awee'; Lauder's 'Saftest o the Family'; Will Fyffe's 'Daft Sandy'), this kind of sketch worked through some of the confusions of rapid cultural change. In 'His First Night Out', Dave Hunter, a sophisticated, up-to-date English speaker, introduces Gordon playing 'Jimmy' (who is awkward, stuttering, old-fashioned) to modern nightlife. The sketch starts with Hunter arranging to meet his girlfriend. Jimmy comes round to look in before

he goes to bed at ten to nine. Hunter is shocked that this 21 year-old should be in bed so early. But, as Jimmy explains: 'It's ma mither, she's aw-fae religious and wants tae bring me up in the proper way.' Hunter decides that it is time Jimmy kicked over the traces. Confusion ensues when Jimmy tries his first cigarette and is then persuaded to go to the pictures:

Hunter: ... *You sit down and in front of you, you will see a big white sheet.*
Gordon: *Oh, I ken whit that is. We've got wan at hame. Its on the bed during the week, and on Sundays it's a table cloth.*
Hunter: *And presently you will see things start to move on that sheet.*
Gordon: *That's right, we've got that at hame an a'.*
Hunter: *Yes, yes, but I mean great big things.*
Gordon: *Oh, you should see our ones.*
Hunter: *Yes, but these things creep across the sheet like this.*
Gordon: *Creep? Our ones lowp.*
Hunter: *Aw, you don't understand. These things are dressed like Cowboys and Indians.*
Gordon: *Oh, ours move sae fast ye canna see how they're dressed.*
Hunter: *Yes, yes, but they're on horseback.*
Gordon: *Oh, ours hanna got that length yet.*
Hunter: *And nowadays, we even have them that can talk.*

Tommy Morgan started out in the 1920s with partner Tommy Yorke.
Highly regarded as a natural exponent of 'Glasgow humour', one of
his best-loved roles was Big Beenie, a larger than life blonde always in
search of a man, who, when she eventually landed an American GI,
became 'Big Beenie the GI bride'. Like several other comedians,
Morgan also ran his own shows (in Portobello in the 1930s, and then in
a 19-season run at the Glasgow Pavilion).

Gordon: *Talk? Oh …*
Hunter: *Of course, they're only pictures. For instance, one of them couldn't come down and say to me 'Will you have a drink?'.*
Gordon: *Oh, well ours are different. Every time I see one of ours, I get a nip.*

Hunter gets Jimmy drunk before introducing him to his 'saucy' girlfriend, but when Hunter tells the girl to come out, Jimmy discovers 'Crickey, it's ma mither!' Nothing is quite what it seems in this sketch, even 'mither' has mutated into a smoking, drinking 'real sport'.

Though the inept gowk seems to be held up for laughs, comedy is rarely so straightforward. Smooth-talking Hunter may possess the allure of the new, but in this sketch, and in the many other re-workings of the same theme, the local insider gets audience sympathy as he deflates his 'better-spoken', up-to-date friend by turning everything he says upside down. This de-bunking by a regional clown, which remains a key technique in the Scots comic armoury, was in a tradition stretching back to antiquity and was only one of many such elements found in the most apparently modern of sketches.

This mixing of the venerable, conservative, familiar and often sentimentally nostalgic with dashes of satire, topicality and novelty, enabled comedians to bridge the gap between the everyday world and sense of shared identity of their audiences and the rapidly evolving world 'outside'. The ability to constantly re-invent this formula kept these comics popular right up until the variety theatres closed down. Indeed, with the rise of touring revues in the 1930s, and then the long-running resident shows of the 1940s and '50s, the best of them could command substantial salaries of up to £500 a week. Tommy Morgan (who had 19 summer residencies at the Glasgow Pavilion) and his successor, Lex McLean, were in the powerful position of being able to supply complete shows to theatres on a 60/40 per cent basis in their favour. (Indeed, McLean is known to have had shares in the theatre.) This was an arrangement that suited theatres, keen to spread the risk in the increasingly chilly 1950s, and it meant that comedians dominated the business. Writing in 1964, the journalist A D Mackie observed that comics preferred to forget the small seaside shows where they had learned their trade:

> … *Scotch comics like to appear in the big theatres, run big cars, be able to talk in terms of hundreds a week. The status is more important than the money, but the money makes the status. So comedians have been known to exaggerate what they were earning ….*

But the 'Decline – and imminent fall – of the Scotch Comic' was already evident to the writer of a 1948 article on the subject, noting that comedians were getting complacent with their six-month seasons and pantomimes, lazily rehashing each other's work. In his opinion they needed better and fresher material if they were to compete with cinema (television was yet to come for most people) and the live American performers who were appearing in top theatres.

A late 1940s Dunoon summer season sketch produced by Alec Finlay, entitled 'Lend-Lease' (after the US war-time policy of helping to arm their allies), makes the point. A GI American tells Scottish sailor Finlay that he needs to get some speed in his chat-up. Patter follows comparing how quickly they can build houses in the USA as opposed to Dunoon, and when Finlay complains that since Americans came over it is impossible to get girlfriends, the American offers advice, successfully demonstrating his 'technique' on an English-speaking 'Modern Miss'. Finlay tries it out on the next girl who, it turns out, works in a pickle factory, speaks with a droning exaggerated 'Glasgow' voice, and thinks that the comically inept Finlay is after her fish supper. The sketch tries to be snappy and Americanised. However, it falls back on an exceedingly well-worn if updated comic wooing formula. This has more in common with nineteenth-century chapbook sketches, re-worked in John Alexander's 1892 comic recitations and sketches like 'Bashfu' Jock', and recorded in the 1930s by, among others, Cissie Lang and Wullie Lindsay as 'A Scotch Wooing'. It ends with the sort of 'auld Scots song' parody which could have been heard 50 or more years earlier.

George Johnstone remembers what was for him a pivotal experience in the mid '50s, playing in Paisley: during a Monday morning cast discussion about what was going into the show, the comic who was appearing asked the stage manager how long it was since 'The Marrying of Mary', a very well-known sketch, had been done. Told that it was done the week before, the comic's response was, 'Ach, I do it differently'. For George, that was the moment he realised that showbusiness in the Galts circuit, which latterly accounted for most of the variety theatre business in Scotland, was finished.

The generation that began their careers after World War II present a more diverse picture. Top performers like Johnny Beattie, Jimmy Logan, Jack Milroy and Larry Marshall, in the last crop to serve the same season after season variety apprenticeships as their pre-war colleagues, carried over much from the established music-hall/variety tradition. They did well in the remaining summer seasons, pantomimes and Howard and Wyndham 'Five Past Eight Shows', where they were joined (particularly in pantomime, which had always seen the heaviest traffic between legit and non-legit) by actors like Stanley Baxter, Rikki Fulton, Duncan MacRae and Molly Urquhart.

Increasingly, however, they had to turn to work in radio, television, clubs, overseas tours, and, pioneered by Larry Marshall, one-man shows. This meant a shift in performance style. A weekly broadcast performance was not the same as twice-weekly live. Stand-up comedy (single, front of curtain comedian reciting gag after gag), the staple of club and cabaret venues, did not offer the same dramatic scope as song and patter and sketch comedy. Although a variety veteran like Lex McLean achieved large television audiences, he was never as comfortable in front of a camera as in his long-running Glasgow Pavilion and Edinburgh Palladium shows, yelling out asides and ad-libs about latecomers.

Was this the end of the Scotch Comic? 'Scotch Comic' is one of those terms that can mean more or less whatever the user wants. It was a stage-role used by a wide range of performers, always being adapted and re-invented. Many pros happily lifted material from visiting English and American stars and saw themselves as comedians with a Scottish accent, rather than

'Scotch Comics' (which for them meant being like Harry Lauder). Nevertheless, posterity has come to see them as 'Scotch Comics' and they all to varying degrees borrowed from their predecessors. Chic Murray, with his pensive monologues, or more recently Billy Connolly, who came from the folk-music scene of the 1960s, seem to owe little to the same tradition as Harry Lauder or Will Fyffe, yet their stage-personae have resonated with the century and a half tradition of comic-Scots who had gone before.

Will Fyffe as the Engineer. Character comedian Will Fyffe started out in his father's portable fit-up theatre at the turn of the century (*see page 114*). By the 1930s he was an international stage, film and recording success with character studies such as the ship's engineer in 'Sailing up the Clyde', 'The Engineer' and (though he was from Dundee) 'I belong to Glasgow'.

Glasgow Empire interior during demolition, May 1963. There had been a
music hall on this site since the Gaiety was built in 1874. This was replaced in 1896
with the larger Empire Palace, with further alterations in 1930 resulting in a capacity of 2100.
In the 1950s a string of top American bookings drew the crowds. (Scottish Media Group)

CLOSURES, CLUBS AND CABARET

The steady trickle of theatre closures and conversions since the 1920s turned into a spate in the late 1950s: Leith Gaiety (1956), Greenock Empire (1957), Dunfermline Opera House and Falkirk Roxy (1958), Paisley Theatre (1959), Edinburgh Empire (1962), Glasgow Empire (1963), Aberdeen Tivoli (1966), Edinburgh Palladium (1968) and the Glasgow Alhambra (1969). The Collins Variety agency closed in 1957, and Galts ten years later.

The main culprit was television, particularly when set ownership became widespread and commercial stations arrived. This alone would have killed off most of the theatre business, but combined with the moving of people from city-centre neighbourhoods within walking distance of theatres to outlying schemes, the decline was inevitable. Even before the final closures people knew because, according to May Morrison,

... theatres like Falkirk and Hamilton Hippodrome they were only doing maybe Fridays or Saturdays. Our summer seasons here [Cragburn] the orchestras had gone. You know, you had maybe four or five of you .... Anywhere you went, there was a pianist that was all. If you were lucky you had two pianists. But most times it was one bashin out the ... but the whole atmosphere had ..., it was just down and down and down. And instead of six [chorus] girls you had four. No the same acts at all. You'd maybe get one name ... just a deterioration.

As managements in the smaller theatres cut back on orchestras, casts, costumes, scenery, maintenance and the number of performances, a downward spiral had set in. A generation gap was opening between youngsters wanting to see rock and roll stars, and their parents who wanted

more familiar variety fare. Older comedians began to seem out of date, and those who tried to appear contemporary with 'bluer' material risked alienating the family audience that was the bedrock of the business.

Summer-season work lingered longer than city centre variety. *The Stage*'s 1973 round-up of summer shows listed productions in 20 towns and cities around Scotland, including several full-scale shows running for weeks (months in the case of the Ayr 'Gaiety Whirl', the last to be run under the Popplewells). The reviews, however, painted a mixed picture, with talk of 'rising costs and dwindling attendance':

> A wave of fresh ideas is needed in resident shows … and this one relies too much on comedy in the old format – Scots kitchen backcloth, table, two chairs, arguing man and wife …. This will never attract the potential, such as there may be, in new variety-fans.

In 1983 the summer-season listing has shows only in Girvan (three nights), Perth and Ayr. In resorts and holiday spots, cabaret-style shows took over in clubs like Archie McCulloch's 'Cumbrae Club' in Millport (opened in 1961), holiday camps, and hotels. The latter were aimed increasingly at visitors from abroad, with a good dose of generic Scottish song, music and tartanry, such as Jamie's 'Scottish Evening' in Edinburgh's King James Hotel, hosted by Larry Marshall for 19 years from the early 1970s:

At the start of the show, when I did the welcome .... I had songs that linked these things about the nationalities and where you're coming from and I went through the entire world .... I would do about ten or twelve minutes there, welcoming the audience .... What followed me was music, was dancing and I was back on again, and then I did a spot with the trio, in which I introduced them .... The next thing I did the ceremony of the Haggis. Interval. After the interval I went on and just for the sake of breaking up the music, the pipes, the dancing, I did just a few gags ... the wee classic spot of the classic Scottish couthy, very funny stories. Three or four minutes. Off. Back to dancing, sing, bit of pipes or trio, whatever. Then I'm back on again to the end. And I do forty minutes and I have four, sometimes five people on stage .... I interview them and turn them into a clan chief by seeing who, with the most style, can get themselves dressed as a clan chief. But I don't make the mistake of using a kilt because that turns them into a fool. I don't make the mistake of using a hat, because that musses up their hair and a lot of Americans wear hair-pieces .... All they did was put on a belt, beautiful big belt, with the sword and a scabbard, over the shoulder and down the left-hand side ... they were shown how to pick up the targ, through the handle and the last thing the Scottish standard on the spear. So all they had to do was put on the belt, pick up the targ, the standard and shout 'Gregarlach', the battle cry of the clan MacGregor, 'Gregarlach' .... It looks very good actually, and a hell of a lot of fun in it. And some of them couldnae get a word; ... I could get two minutes out of trying to get a Japanese man to say 'Gregarlach' ... That was ten to twelve minutes of that, followed by a song for every nationality in the room with them doing the singing .... Then I finished up doing a very short spot. I think I did 'I love a Lassie', 'Loch Lomond', and one other and into the finale, 'Keep right on to the end of the road' .... Six nights a week ... and I loved it.

By the mid 1960s, despite the efforts of performers like Jimmy Logan with the Glasgow Metropole (formerly the Empress) and Calum Kennedy with the Dundee Palace and Aberdeen Tivoli, it was no longer possible for most acts to make a year-round living in the fewer, shorter summer and pantomime seasons, and few nights of touring revues hosted in the remaining variety theatres and civic venues. Performers had to look elsewhere.

Re-workings of the 'all-Scottish' variety shows were presented on television, compèred by singers or comedians and with a more intimate 'ceilidh' format suitable for the cameras. But since

Hector Nicol and Glen Daly.
Hector Nicol started his 52-year career in variety before the World War II, first as a solo singer, then with a successful cowboy act, The Rodeo Three. After the war he worked as a feed, including 16 years with Johnny Victory, before turning to his own brand of character comedy in the clubs. According to his widow Lena, 'Nobody since ... could fill the clubs like he did'. Compere and singer Glen Daly, 'Mr Glasgow', another variety theatre graduate, is shown outside the Ashfield Club (run by Jimmy Donald, owner of the Ashfield greyhound track) where he recorded several high-selling LPs in the late 1960s and early '70s.

it only took one show with a dozen or so performers to reach hundreds of thousands, television opportunities were scarce. In any case, by the 1980s this Indian summer was (apart from Hogmanay shows) over, as the blend of kilts, 'auld Scots songs' and Scottish country dancing fell out of favour with producers.

For those who missed out on television, the development in the 1950s of social and working men's clubs with a purpose-built stage for hosting cabaret offered other opportunities. To an extent this type of work continued the soirée tradition which had been so lucrative for Victorian pros, but on a new scale following the lead of large, well-funded working men's clubs in the north of England, the wealthiest of which might fly over an American singer for the night. Singers and stand-up comedians were the main beneficiaries of club work. Performers like 'King of Clubland' Hector Nicol or singer Glen Daly alternated between club work and the remaining theatre work. But many performers, like Billy Crockett, who had been working in theatres since the late 1930s, found 'it was harder when entertainment moved into clubs'. Instead of weeks or months of work, they tended only to offer one night stands:

One time you'd be down in Cardiff, the next night you'd be in Newcastle and so sometimes you'd to do three hundred odd miles in the night … and when you were in variety shows you only used to do about ten minutes or twelve minutes at the most … the clubs wanted you to do half an hour, forty minutes, fifty minutes and then said would you go on twice … you couldn't ask an acrobat to do half an hour, the fellow would kill himself wouldn't he, turning summersaults and that. So, not many acts made the changeover but I managed to bridge the gap after a while. Oh, but clubs were hard to play. You used to go on in some clubs and they were all drinking and talking to one another and somebody would say 'the pies are comin': half-a-dozen of the people left the audience and you were left talking to yourself. And the one-armed bandit was going, the cash register was going, whereas when you were playing the theatre the people could only sit there and eat sweets and watch you.

Many variety veterans found far richer pickings further afield, particularly among the nostalgically minded ex-patriate Scottish communities of Australia, North America and New Zealand which had been hosting Scottish entertainers for well over a century. Alec Finlay was one of many entertainers to tour widely in Canada and elsewhere, a tradition carried on by Ronnie Coburn, a former stage carpenter turned feed in Finlay's tours, and veteran of over three decades of touring with his own 'Breath of Scotland' company.

Openings for many acts were more limited. As Billy Crockett suggests above, the smaller-scale venues did not have the facilities for physical or acrobatic acts. The descendants of the more eccentric specialities, however, can still be found entertaining at childrens' parties and other private functions, or in the world of corporate and promotional entertainment. A new breed of 'Entertainment agency' supplies a range of amusements that, in the words of one listing, reads like part fairground entertainers and novelty attractions, part circus and variety acts:

Magician – Clowns – Jugglers – Stiltwalkers – Puppet Shows – Caricaturists – Face Painters – Bands – Discos – Comperes – Karaoke – Bungee Running – Bucking Bronco – Fly Wall – Gladiators – Bouncy Castle – Bouncy Boxing – Sumo Inflatable – Maze – Giant Slides – Quad Bikes – Waltzers Wheel – Lazer Clays & Much More …

Although many of the ingredients that went into music hall and variety theatre in Scotland can still be found, a night at the Palladium or Pavilion was always more than the sum of its parts, not the least of which was the very act of going week after week to a well-known and loved neighbourhood venue for an evening's communal entertainment.

That this has gone is reflected both in the revivalist flavour of the remaining shows, and also in the gradual elevation of music hall and variety into the pantheon Scottish heritage, *ie* something belonging to the past. Cultural commentators 100 years ago saw music hall as a threat to 'true' Scottish culture, and more recent writers saw its often unfettered tartanalia as highly pathological, but over the past decade or so museums have been actively acquiring memorabilia and mounting exhibitions.

Arguably Scotland's most consistent theatrical tradition is its popular theatre, with comedians and singers in particular maintaining a distinctive Scottish lineage. However, the idea of a Scottish music-hall tradition can be limiting. It obscures how much showbusiness went on outside the music halls and theatres and instead focuses too narrowly on those elements that played up a sense of shared 'Scottish' identity. In reality, the popular stage always overlapped with the legitimate, and was hungry for the new and cosmopolitan. Much that appeared in theatres, particularly the number ones and twos, could be found across the United Kingdom and abroad; the acts which were most popular in Scotland were often not 'Scottish' at all, and many of the most successful Scottish

performers pursued careers on an international stage. That music hall and variety theatre thrived for so long in Scotland was due largely to the ability of performers, producers and impresarios to adapt to changes in the wider world whilst fostering a sense of continuity and community. This kept audiences singing the same 'auld Scots songs' of life in the glens, generations after their forebears had first crowded into the cities and into the glittering new palaces of entertainment.

Singer and dancer Sally Foy.

FURTHER READING AND LISTENING, AND PLACES TO VISIT

GENERAL HISTORIES

J H Littlejohn, *The Scottish Music Hall, 1880-1990,* (Wigtownshire, 1990), a thorough gazetteer of theatres and performers. Jack House, *Music Hall Memories: Recollections of Scottish Music Hall and Pantomime* (Glasgow, 1986), Gordon Irving, *The Good Auld Days; the Story of Scotland's Entertainers from Music Hall to Television* (London, 1977) and Albert Mackie, *The Scotch Comedians* (Edinburgh, 1973) are all based on the authors' experiences as theatre journalists.

MUSIC HALL AND BEFORE

The Life of Billy Purvis, the Extraordinary, Witty and Comical Showman (Newcastle Upon Tyne, 1981, first published 1875) and *The Life of a Showman: to Which is Added, Managerial Struggles, by David Prince Miller, Late of the Adelphi Theatre, Glasgow* (London & Leeds, 1849) both give vivid accounts of the decades before music hall. For the music hall era the best source is Daniel Barr's *Professional Gazette and Advertiser* (held in the Mitchell Library, Glasgow) published in Glasgow under various names over the last decades of the nineteenth century. Eye-witness accounts include Glasgow concert promoter Walter Freer's *My Life and Memories* (Glasgow, 1929), comedian Willie Frame's *W. F. Frame Tells his Own Story* (Glasgow, 1907), James Houston, *Autobiography of Mr. James Houston, Scotch Comedian* (Glasgow & Edinburgh, 1889), Harry Lauder, *Harry Lauder at Home and on Tour* (London, 1907) and *Roamin' in the Gloamin'* (London, 1928), J Wilson McLaren's mainly theatrical *Edinburgh Memories and some Worthies* (Edinburgh & London, 1926) and James Scott Skinner, *My Life and Adventures* (Aberdeen 1994, reprinted from *The People's Journal,* 1923).

VARIETY AND AFTER

F Bruce, A Foley & G Gillespie (eds), *Those Variety Days* (Edinburgh, 1997), F Bruce & A Foley (eds), *More Variety Days* (Edinburgh, 2000) and Vivien Devlin's *Kings, Queens and People's Palaces: an Oral History of the Scottish Variety Theatre, 1920-1970* (Edinburgh, 1991), all contain wide-ranging recollections of the business. Biographies and reminiscences include Priscilla Barlow's account of Duncan Macrae's career, *Wise Enough to Play the Fool* (Edinburgh, 1995), Stanley Baxter with Alex Mitchell, *Stanley Baxter's Bedside Book of Glasgow Humour* (London, 1986), Rikki Fulton, *Is it That Time Already* (Edinburgh, 1999), Renée Houston, *Don't Fence Me In* (London, 1974), broadcaster Howard Lockhart's *On My Wavelength* (Aberdeen, 1973), Jimmy Logan, *It's a Funny Life* (Edinburgh, 1998), Josette Collins Marchant, *Journey Through Stageland; the Collins Family of Glasgow* (Wigtown, 1996), impresario Archie McCulloch's *Shoot-out at Auchenshuggle; Archie McCulloch's Own Story* (Glasgow, 1991), Dorothy Paul, *Revelations of a Rejected Soprano* (London, 1997), Frank Wappit, *Master Joe Petersen* (North Shields, 1994), Iain Watson, *Harry Gordon; 'The Laird of Inversnecky'* (Aberdeen, 1993), Andrew Yule, *The Chic Murray Story* (Edinburgh, 1989).

For individual theatres see J H Littlejohn, *The Tivoli Theatre Aberdeen* (Edinburgh, 2000), John Moore, *Ayr Gaiety; The Theatre Made Famous by the Popplewells* (Edinburgh, 1976) and Jim Pratt, *His Majesty's Theatre; A Short History* (Aberdeen, 1987).

THE WIDER CONTEXT

P Bailey (ed), *Music Hall: the Business of Pleasure* (Milton Keynes, 1986), J S Bratton (ed), *Music Hall: Performance and Style* (Milton Keynes, 1986), Bruce Peter, *Scotland's Splendid Theatres* (Edinburgh, 1999), A Cameron & A Scullion (eds), *Scottish Popular Theatre and Entertainment: Historical and Critical Approaches to Theatre and Film in Scotland*, (Glasgow, 1996), Bill Findlay (ed), *A History of Scottish Theatre* (Edinburgh, 1998), Gerald Frow, '*Oh, yes it is'; A History of Pantomime* (London, 1985), Dagmar Kift, *The Victorian Music Hall: Culture, Class and Conflict* (Cambridge, 1996), Karen Marshalsay (ed), *The Waggle o' the Kilt: Popular Theatre and Entertainment in Scotland* (Glasgow, 1992), G J Mellor, *The Northern Music Hall* (Newcastle Upon Tyne, 1970), and Roger Wilmut, *Kindly Leave the Stage!; the Story of Variety 1919-1960* (London, 1985).

RECORDINGS

Though they lack the atmosphere of live performance the hundreds of recordings made by Scottish music hall and variety theatre singers, comedians and musicians are a valuable resource, beginning with W F Frame's in the first ever recording session in Glasgow. Recordings by Harry Lauder sold millions around the world (and have been released on various CD compilations) but more locally orientated 78 recordings by many other Scottish performers were released by the Beltona and Parlophone labels from the 1920s-'50s. Useful compilations are Seil Recordings' (Rothesay) archive series of Will Fyffe (SEV3 & SEV12), Harry Gordon (SEBC7 & SEV16) and various artists on 'Remember When …' Volumes 1 & 2 (SEV18 & SEV19).

PLACES TO VISIT

Aberdeen – Tivoli Theatre (whose future is uncertain – contact Celia Walker, Aberdeen Tivoli Theatre Steering Group, 41 Rubislaw Park Crescent, Aberdeen, AB15 8BT).

Ayr – Gaiety (now run by the local authority).

Edinburgh – Festival Theatre (formerly Edinburgh Empire) and King's Theatre.

Glasgow – Citizen's Theatre (formerly the Princess' Theatre), King's Theatre, Pavilion Theatre, and the Britannia/Panopticon Theatre (awaiting planned restoration having been used as a warehouse) – contact The Britannia Music Hall Trust, 113-117, Trongate, Glasgow, G1 5HD.

Largs – Barrfield's Pavilion (restored as an entertainments venue).

Rothesay – Winter Gardens (administered by a trust and now housing a restaurant and cinema).

Significant holdings relating to music hall and variety theatre are held by the National Library of Scotland, Edinburgh, Mitchell Library, Glasgow, People's Palace Museum, Glasgow, Scottish Screen and the Scottish Theatre Archive at Glasgow University Library (see their web page on http://special.lib.gla.ac.uk/STA/staindex.html). Other websites of interest are those of the Glasgow Pavilion, (http://www.paviliontheatre.co.uk), the Krankies, (http://www.thekrankies.cwc.net) and the self-explanatory http://www.sirharrylauder.com.

The Scottish Music Hall Society organises regular talks and events and produces a regular newsletter. It can be contacted through the Secretary at 69 Langmuirhead Road, Auchinloch, Kirkintilloch, G66 5DJ.